STICKING TO
MY STORY

THE ALCHEMY OF STORYTELLING FOR STARTUPS

DONNA GRIFFIT

PUBLISHING

Sticking to My Story: The Alchemy of Storytelling for Startups

Copyright © 2023 by Donna Griffit.

For information contact :

ATG Publishing

info@atgpublishing.com - http://www.atgpublishing.com

ISBN: 9781991197313

First Edition: February 2023

10 9 8 7 6 5 4 3 2 1

CONTENTS

Contents 3

Dedication 3

Foreword by Tim Draper 5

Intro - My Origin Story 9

    Corporate Storytelling 9

    "Starting Up" a New Story................................. 10

Food, Water, Oxygen and …Stories? - Why Stories are a Vital
Human Need 13

    The Historical Significance of Storytelling 14

The Building "Chunks" of Storytelling for Investors 21

    The 4 Acts or "Chunks" of a Startup Pitch Deck 24

    Before you go any further, ask yourself if you're REALLY
    ready to raise.. 25

The Guide to Practical Startup Storytelling 31

    The Overture.. 32

    Act I - The Problem (aka The Villain) 47

    Act II - The Solution (aka The Hero) 70

    Act III - The Biz (aka the Hero's Action Plan)........... 91

Act IV - Moving Forward (aka The Hero's Next Moves) 134

A Note About Slides 143

Upping Your Pitch Game - The polish that makes the
difference...147

Now that you have the Perfect Pitch Deck - How to get VC
meetings..148

Tips for Peak Performance Presenting 159

The Elevator Pitch - Be ready to pitch in a pinch...............165

Q&A - It might be more important than the pitch! 169

Epic Pitch Fails - The biggest mistakes startups make - and
what to do instead 189

Final Thoughts - What's the Future of Storytelling for
Startups 195

About the Author 203

References: 205

DEDICATION

To Brad Boyer, aka Mr. Bleu, who saw the potential in me before I saw it in myself.

To my Mom, Madeline, who has always been my biggest champion and believer.

To Jonny, my constant, the wind in my sails, and my partner in everything.

And to Lily and Emma, who showed me the true magic of storytelling through their eyes.

FOREWORD BY TIM DRAPER

Tim Draper's Top 5 Tips for Entrepreneurs

1 — Delight your customer
2 — Hire Carefully
3 — Fail and fail again
4 — Know how to reach your customers
5 — The best ideas are simple
Bonus — Attend Draper University

And an additional bonus tip - when fundraising - tell a story. A story that will captivate investors, paint a visionary picture far beyond what you're doing today - and of course, a story worth millions - sorry - billions.

One of the reasons that we created Draper U was to give youth from around the world the opportunity to go to "Entrepreneur School." We wanted to let them drink from the Silicon Valley cooler, be inspired and then take these ideas home and grow them into thriving companies.

One of the stations that founders pass is being able to pitch their company in five minutes and even one minute.

You see, if it takes longer than that to capture the essence of what you do, you've lost me. Tell a great story, and I can listen to you for hours.

I can't tell you how many terrible, horrible pitches I've seen over my decades of investing. Sometimes it's so bad that my eyes bleed and my ears burn; I literally want to pull my hair out. Why do entrepreneurs put us through such misery?

Well, finally, there are no more excuses. "Sticking to My Story" is the new bible for startup founders. It's the A-Z recipe for how to create a powerful pitch deck with all the right ingredients. It's filled with helpful tips and fascinating stories of what worked and what failed abysmally, peppered with insightful quotes from my colleagues in Silicon Valley.

Donna Griffit has worked with Draper Ventures on some of our pitch decks, as well as coaching students in Draper U. She is a masterful storyteller with an incredible capacity to rapidly ingest data and spit it out in the form of a magical pitch. If you've ever seen her coach pitch after pitch, it's nothing short of mesmerizing.

And now Donna, after nearly 20 years of helping Founders write winning pitches that have raised over a billion dollars, is letting you into the inner sanctum of her method. If you are raising funding or plan to be raising funding, get a copy of this book yesterday.

Intro - My Origin Story

I always tell my clients to start with their origin story - it lends credibility and "hooks" people in. (We'll discuss more on how to do this later in the book). I always try to eat my own dog food - or better yet - drink my own champagne (definitely more attractive than dog food!), so here's my origin story:

Corporate Storytelling

In 2003, when I finally decided what I wanted to be when I grew up, fresh out of Grad school, I answered an ad on Craigslist looking for Corporate Trainers for Presentation Skills and Business Writing Skills workshops. It was a pivotal moment in my life, for it was then I met the man that would change my life – Brad Boyer of Boyer Communications Group. Under his mighty wing, I learned to help people take bits and bytes, technobabble and terminology, unwind them, and craft clear, compelling messages that drove people to action. Whether the goal was sales, marketing, pushing a technological change, or even a VP level Keynote Speech. I traveled from Santa Clara, California, to Shanghai, China and everywhere in between, working with Fortune 500 companies in the fields of Silicon Chips, Potato Chips, and even Chocolate Chips.

It was a joy spending time with these people and seeing them make magnificent breakthroughs in a 1-3 day workshop. I have kept in touch with participants from all over the world, whom I now call friends. Though each local culture had its own flavor, I came to learn that no matter where I was in the world, as human beings, we all share the tendency to over-tell a story, we all suffer from stage fright at varying degrees and times, and we all struggle to sell our own value. It was a privilege to help my participants break through the boundaries that were holding them back.

"STARTING UP" A NEW STORY

In 2008 I found myself in unfamiliar territory – the deck had been shuffled – literally – and with the economic downturn, organizations were cutting any training that wasn't considered "vital" – and apparently, the skills required to sell an idea or a product didn't make the cut. I was baffled and bewildered – what would I do next? I had never held a "typical" 9-5 job, I had owned my businesses since I was 7 when I became a clown for birthday parties, and I had no idea where to start.

As serendipity would have it, I was handed my next pivotal moment. A friend connected me to a prominent Cardiothoracic surgeon who needed help with his speaking abilities. He also happened to have two medical device startups with which he needed help with his fundraising pitches.

Though I had never worked on an "investor pitch" before, my years of experience had taught me that a story is a story, and, when told in the right way, can drive action and captivate audiences of any type. After working with him for several months, I attended an Angel Conference where I presented on his behalf. I saw other companies that were invited to present at this prestigious forum come ill-prepared, and as I watched them painfully get shot down by investors, I knew I had found my new audience.

I fell in love with the world of startups and founders, of telling high-stake stories that raised millions of dollars, and of helping brilliant minds once again unwind the technobabble into meaningful messages that drove to action. Since 2009, my focus has been startup storytelling – investor decks, sales decks, competition pitches, explainer videos – anything that startups need to tell a powerful story to a specific audience - fast!

My sincere belief is that everyone has a story that is unique and compelling. There are no boring stories – there are merely layers and stacks of information piled up, obscuring the beauty of the story. I'm here to help peel the layers away and let startups polish their stories until they "shine like the top of the Chrysler building" I'm honored and humbled to work every day with companies that are genuinely changing the world and excited to have a part in their journey.

Stewart Butterfield, CEO of Slack, said:

"A piece of advice I'd give my younger self: concentrate on the storytelling, on convincing people. If you can't do that, it doesn't matter how good the product is."

The Founder of one of the most prominent Silicon Valley startups said it - so it must be true.

So how do you concentrate on the storytelling piece? How do you organize your data in a clear way that grabs your audience's attention? How do you convince them that you are the next big thing and get funded? This book will serve as a very practical guide for doing just that. Let's go!

Food, Water, Oxygen and ...Stories? - Why Stories are a Vital Human Need

I recently attended the concert of a certain Sir Paul McCartney. Being an avid Beatles fan, I couldn't resist taking my young daughters to see the concert of an actual Beatle! One day, when they understood the magnitude, they'd have some significant bragging rights!

The music was fantastic, and the lighting and sound were spectacular - Paul, at 79, had all the Joie De Vivre and energy he did back in the day. But what made the night truly unforgettable were the stories he told between the songs. Paul held 20,000 people in the palm of his hand as he regaled us with vignettes and anecdotes of the Beatles years. We laughed, we cried, we collectively gasped, and most of all, we sat on the edge of our seats like a group of kindergarteners at storytime.

This is the magic of storytelling.

Were the stories 100% true? Maybe... Did it matter? No! Paul told them with such charm and conviction that we were persuaded, and all of us can retell his stories to other Beatles fans, adding to our repertoire of useless trivia.

THE HISTORICAL SIGNIFICANCE OF STORYTELLING

Storytelling - it is one of the hottest buzzwords today. Everyone is saying that you must know how to be a good storyteller – but does anyone really know what that means?

People often misunderstand the idea of storytelling – they think it means that they should just stand around telling anecdotes, insert a meaningless joke or "dumb down" weighty materials, making them look stupid or silly. On the contrary!

In his worldwide bestselling book, "Sapiens - A Brief History of Humankind," Yuval Noah Harari reveals that a big reason we outcompeted the neanderthals is because of our ability to tell stories. It meant we could cooperate on a level way beyond what they could and were able to grow exponentially. Even humans thousands of years ago knew that to get people to join their cause, they needed stories. This rings just as true today.

I've seen too many founders think they can flash numbers, data points and techie buzzwords, and people will follow them like sheep, but it ignores our entire human history. The details can help, but they aren't what gets your foot in the door; it's the stories that captivate people.

Take a look at the dating app Bumble, for example. The Founder, Whitney Wolfe-Herd, discovered the online dating world to be an intimidating place for women. She created her own brand with a women-first focus, and it made her the first woman to lead a tech unicorn to IPO. Customers and investors got behind her because of her mission, not the details of exactly how it worked.

You can't assume everyone who you talk to about your business holds a double PhD in Computer Science. If you can't explain what you do in a way that 90% of the adult population will understand, then you've failed to understand what your company does. It's time to go back to the drawing board. Under the covers at Bumble (no pun intended), the algorithms and tech are complex, but most people only care about the end effect, not how it's achieved.

Storytelling has been around for tens of thousands of years. In a Princeton publication called "The Irresistible Fairy Tale: The Cultural and Social History of a Genre" by Jack Zipes, he proposes that we have been telling stories since before we could even speak in words. Though we don't have any actual records of these very early stories which either warned of dangers or set the stage for very early fables and tales, there are visual representations of stories from our late ancestors that prove this point.

Thirty-six thousand years ago, in the Chauvet cave in France, we see what is likely the oldest representation of storytelling discovered to date. The paintings seem to tell the story of a volcanic eruption.

An early story painted in the Chauvet Cave

Egyptian hieroglyphics in approximately 3,000 B.C., mixing symbols and sounds that tell a story, were the next evolution of storytelling, mainly for religious recording and important messages to be passed down to future generations.

In 700 B.C., we finally see stories recorded through language, with the Epic of Gilgamesh and the Iliad by Homer. Recording these stories helped to spread them across the world long before the internet. Other popular stories that were written and recorded during the same period include what we know as Aesop's Fables. It was at this time that we also saw the rise of the use of plays to tell stories, which will be a central theme in this book.

Storytelling was also conveyed through myths, songs, chants and poetry to tell tales passed from generation to generation. This was evident in Native American cultures, such as the creation story of the Cherokee tribe, which has multiple versions that differ from storyteller to storyteller. The fact that humans were able to tell and eventually record these stories is the reason they have remained part of our literary canon for more than 2,000 years.

Around the year 1800, we saw a technological shift that took storytelling to many modalities: photography, movies, telephones, radio, TV, and in more recent years, digital, social and mobile media. Blogs, Twitter, and Facebook now let users have their own personal storytelling platform in the form of status updates, pictures and videos of memories and personal stories. Instagram and TikTok take us full circle back to the earliest days when stories were expressed visually - helping to unleash the primal, visual storyteller in each of us.

Storytelling is the difference between rambling off data and giving it meaning. When we read a good book, we devour it – we feel swept into the story. Time and space fall away – and it's sad to end it because it's like we're saying goodbye to a good friend. We don't look for 100% historical accuracy, technical data or facts and figures – we just give ourselves over to the experience.

Storytelling works very well in the business and tech worlds because:

Our brains can deal with a structured story – while we often struggle to cope with mounds of data.

Stories inspire, captivate and resonate – aren't those the things you want for your business life? (Personal life too!)

And the best thing is, stories are universal – we find storytelling in every culture, religion and geography - so storytelling is an excellent equalizer among different people in different roles.

Studies have shown that our brains don't always distinguish between strong memories and conveyed memories, which can create false memories or inferences. We see this happening often in traditional or familial storytelling, which happens every time a group of people gather for a party, a holiday, or an event.

I'm sure you have a story that your grandparents, parents or a member of your extended family have told you - that happened before you were even born! You may even hear the same story retold every year at every family gathering, and likely you know it verbatim. That story is so alive, so vivid, that you can almost hear the sounds, smell and taste the food, see the happenings unfold. Almost as if you were there!

These stories are so powerful that in our minds, they actually become our own! Our brain can no longer distinguish between stories that are so deeply ingrained in us and occurrences that actually happened, and a new perception of reality is created. And as the famous George Costanza of Seinfeld fame said, "If you believe it, it's not a lie." Perhaps this explains why pathological liars truly believe their lies.

Wait, so when we tell stories, are we lying? Isn't this harmful? Unethical? Well, this can be problematic in certain situations, like if you were to witness a crime and were asked to describe the details of the perpetrator and the circumstances. What actually happened and what we "remember with certainty" as happening can be colored by so many things. Luckily, police are trained to know that any details you give them may be merged with your own storytelling perception, and mistakes still happen, though no malice is intended.

But that's not my proposed use of storytelling. In the case of business and technology, with storytelling, we can simply make powerful inroads into people's perceptions and memory. I will present stories of Founders that I worked with that used stories from their personal lives to motivate the pain they are solving, and it worked beautifully.

Disclaimer - please don't think that I am asking you to lie in your pitches! Not at all - never! If you lie about numbers, metrics, and achievements - you will eventually be found out. (And if you don't believe me, take Elizabeth Homes and Samuel Bankman-Fried's word for it!)

However, using storytelling well gives you the license to mold your message in the best way possible, to shave away the unnecessary details, to make the powerful parts front and center and to "borrow from the future" in a visionary way. With great power comes great responsibility - so use it wisely!

Now that we understand the importance - how do we approach storytelling in our messages?

The Building "Chunks" of Storytelling for Investors

I have two daughters, Lily and Emma. They are in 4th and 1st grade, respectively. It is simply astounding to see their capacity for learning. Their brains are like little sponges that just soak up every drop of knowledge and then come and repeat it back to us. They don't argue with teachers about preconceived notions and debate the merits of numbers vs. letters - they just take it all in. There will be time for critical thinking much later in life.

If you've taken a course, learned a new skill, a language, or gone back to school for an advanced degree in your more mature years, you'll notice that the learning doesn't flow with quite the same ease. Somewhere along the line, our sponges became saturated, and no amount of wringing out will help. Our "hard drives" need a good defrag, our Operating Systems are the equivalent of a Windows 1995 or even DOS. Moreover, as adult humans, we have learned to question, doubt and argue. This so-called "teacher", lecturer or trainer standing at the head of the room is no longer a deity, but rather a person who is equal in our minds, maybe even our junior. And who are they to teach us? So when they say something challenging, confusing, new or wrong in our opinion, our survival instincts kick in, and we either "fight" aka - argue or challenge them to a word sparring contest, or we take "flight" and disengage from what we construe as mindless drivel.

Let's say for a minute that you are that speaker - is that what you want your audience to do? No. But it is not their fault. They simply can't digest so much raw data all at once without fighting or fleeing.

Enter the principle of Chunking. Chunking was introduced in 1956 by George A. Miller in a paper called "The Magical Number Seven, Plus or Minus Two." What Mr. Miller was telling us was there is a formula for the right amount of information to pass on to our audiences:

$$7 +/- 2$$

This means that anything over seven chunks of information - our minds will simply not be able to absorb.

Think about social security numbers, license plate numbers, or especially phone numbers, where you have the country code - area code - first three numbers - second four numbers, all broken into neat little groupings - all grouped into threes and fours. Isn't it MUCH easier to remember +1-867-5309 than 18675309? (By the way, if you call that number, you might get Jenny, and if you're a child of the 80s, you're likely singing along with me right now ;))

Even when you give someone your number, you don't rattle off all the numbers; you intuitively give it to them in a sequence of three, then four.

Think of it this way - if I were writing a book about fresh fruit and I said: "In this book we will discuss different types of fresh fruit: mangoes, melons, apples, pears, plums, strawberries, coconut, and figs." Then I asked you to repeat the list back to me (no peeking!) What would you remember? Figs because it's the last? Plums because it's your favorite? Not likely that you will remember the whole list though.

But if I were to say: "In this book we will discuss different types of fresh fruit: Starting with

Tropical Fruit, which includes: Mangoes, Papayas and Coconut
Moving on to Stone Fruit: Plums, Cherries and Peaches
And for dessert - Pome Fruit: Apples, Pears and Quince.

A bit easier to take a bite out of - I should hope.

So speaking of bites, if we apply the principle of chunking to our presentations - we would "chunk" together similar information into bite-size sections.

Miller said that 7 is the magic number - give or take 2 - I'm saying that the REAL magic number is 4.

Looking back at our history of storytelling, the early greats wrote in "Acts" - Act I, II, III, IV - and so forth. And there was a very intentional structure to it. So we will now be applying this structure to our startup pitch decks.

THE 4 ACTS OR "CHUNKS" OF A STARTUP PITCH DECK

THE NEED
Challenge/Problem

PROPOSED SOLUTION
Product Overview

BUSINESS PLAN
Current Status, Traction,
Team, Biz Model,
Market Opportunity,
Go-to-Market,
Competitive Analysis

VISION FOR FUTURE
Milestones, Products, Funding
Requirements,
ROI, etc

 **KEY INVESTMENT MERITS**

Here are the 4 Chunks (or Acts) of your Startup's Pitch Deck

The Need - The problem, or the "villain" of the story, if you will

The Solution - The "hero" of the story, what will solve the problem and slay the villain?

The Business Plan - What will happen after the hero takes action?

Moving Forward - The aftermath, hoping that the hero is triumphant!

Staying with the theater lingo - there will also be the "Overture", - aka "The Why" or "The Vision Statement", and there will also be an "Epilogue", - otherwise known as "Key Investment Merits." In the next session, we will dive deep into each of these.

BEFORE YOU GO ANY FURTHER, ASK YOURSELF IF YOU'RE REALLY READY TO RAISE.

I'm going to do something a bit counterintuitive now. I'm going to say - maybe this book needs to be parked for a bit. I'm going to ask you to ask yourself a very serious question - are you truly ready to raise? This is not an easy question to answer, but if you aren't ready, stopping now and getting the traction needed to be ready can be the make or break of your fundraise - and your company. If you are not ready to raise, even the best story or storyteller will not be able to tell your story. It would be a bit like trying to cook a gourmet meal when all you have in your fridge is some ketchup, a half-eaten yogurt and some leftover Chinese takeout. No matter how hard you try, a gourmet meal will not be cooked.

Over the years, I've had to stop working with founders on their fundraising pitches. It wasn't because their idea didn't have potential. It wasn't because they weren't great founders. It was because it was obvious to me that their startup was still being prepared for funding.

Too many entrepreneurs are focusing on raising capital as the end goal and forgetting that it's only a means to a greater end. You should be driven by what your startup can achieve with the funding rather than the funding itself. Think of it like a stop at a gas station on a long road trip, and you better buckle up because it's a bumpy road ahead.

TV can make fundraising look so easy. You might have seen an exciting deal close on Shark Tank. You may have thought that fundraising is as simple as going into a room for twenty minutes and coming away with a new business partner and a chunky check. The truth is, fundraising becomes a full-time job for founders and takes over their entire lives.

With the funding frenzy in 2021, some founders were mistakenly led to believe that investors hand out money like hotcakes. In the bleak reality of these starkly different times, investors will only give you something if you can prove you're ready. If you try to fundraise too early, your business idea will be ripped apart, and you'll burn a future bridge for not respecting the investor's time.

The problem when you are a first-time founder is how to know when you're ready. There are three critical aspects to being ready that you need to have nailed down. Then you can start to think about raising funding.

YOU SATISFY A REAL NEED.

There is a potential problem when a startup tries to raise too early. The fact is, the product still needs to be at the stage where it can afford the lack of attention it receives during the fundraising phase. It's not uncommon for a company to digress while the founders are occupied elsewhere. This vicious cycle makes it even harder for the startup to raise money and the founders more desperate.

This means doing the actual work and getting out there to talk to potential customers. Investors will not be impressed if you turn up to a pitch and haven't done as much research as possible. You shouldn't expect them to validate your market for you. You need to talk to as many potential customers as possible about this pain point. You need to validate that it is a pain — that they either lack a solution or the solution they are currently using is missing the mark, and they need something much better. Don't be obsessed with your solution — be obsessed with solving their problem.

Investors might ask you some questions that take you by surprise about other companies who are tackling the same issue that you are. They may ask you what your differentiation is. Do not be caught off guard. Find every single company attempting to solve this pain, whether an enterprise solution or an early-stage startup, know what they're doing and identify how your approach is genuinely different.

You can only adequately explain how your product is differentiated if you have a deep understanding of the struggles your customers go through and the gaps in the existing products. If you can nail this, you are ready to seek investment.

HAVE AN MVP OR BEYOND

Most founders should put in more sweat equity before seeking investment from external sources. Instead of investing the bulk of your precious time on fundraising, roll up your sleeves, dig deep, and work on creating an MVP — or minimum viable product. Have something that works on a basic level or beyond to show investors.

What were the conversations you had with potential customers about the pain? Now come back to them and see what kind of product they fantasize about. Build your product with them in mind, and have them come on as design partners. They can then be early adopters that will fall so deeply in love with your product that they will convert into paying users. And having lots of paying users is the best way to persuade investors that you are a great investment prospect.

YOUR PLAN IS EXECUTABLE.

The final piece of the puzzle is whether your idea can realistically give investors the level of return they expect. You need to remember that most startups will fail, so the potential upside must be massive for it to be worth taking the risk.

I turn down working with many founders because their ideas are simply not venture-scale businesses. Not to say that they can't be very nice lifestyle businesses and make their founders a significant income. But they can't scale to a venture-level business. You can't use a small sample and then extrapolate to say you'll be a hit worldwide. This is especially true if your home country or market is tiny. Even if you've got customers who love you and pay you on your home turf, you must have a plan of how you will penetrate major markets and compete with the big players.

You should avoid going to a fundraising pitch with the vague idea of wanting to expand overseas. You should come armed with clear next steps and with which markets you will target first and why. Then, critically, you need to explain to them how their money will help you reach your next milestone/s.

Also, before you consider fundraising, you should have the right team in place to manage the company effectively in your absence or when you're busy fundraising. You need to trust these people with all your heart. In your pitches, it's not just you under the microscope but the team as well. If you can pull together a group of superstars, everything becomes more manageable.

Venture capitalists expect you to need multiple funding rounds to reach the big end goal. One Silicon Valley venture partner said to me, "Once I write a check, I'm on the hook to help them raise their next round. Having clarity on what they will achieve in the next 18 months is super important for me to see how you'll raise your next round and how I'll onboard the best investors for you."

If you can tell them what you hope to achieve in this round and where you will be positioned after, you prove to them that you're ready for funding. If you don't meet these criteria yet — that's okay! Just get to work and accomplish as much as you can before you hit the roadshow.

THE GUIDE TO PRACTICAL STARTUP STORYTELLING

One thing I have learned over nearly two decades of working with startups is that the most precious commodity Founders have is TIME. You cannot buy time; you're on a race against the clock to get your product funded, to market, to product/market fit, funded again - lather, rinse, repeat. Founders will often reach out to me after 37 iterations and 187 hours spent working and reworking a pitch deck, still not getting the meetings or the funding they need from potential investors. Then they spend 2 hours with me, and we crack it. I want to save you those hundreds of hours and help you crack it too. Therefore, I have boiled my method down to a science, and made it SUPER practical - and this is my secret recipe that I will now share with you.

THE OVERTURE

In a Broadway play, you'll have the orchestra playing the overture of the music before the curtain rises, or in a good movie where there's a scene that happens as a teaser before the opening credits, grabbing your attention and keeping you engaged. This should also be true for your pitch deck. You have a few things to take care of before you even dive into the story itself that can have them onboard before you even start the pitch (cue the Orchestra).

WHAT THEY'RE REALLY LISTENING FOR

In my experience, there are three things investors really pay attention to throughout the entire pitch.

Credibility – This is where your numbers and preparation come into play. You need to show them you know what you're talking about with evidence to back up your words, and hopefully with a stellar team of experts with unique knowledge and experience in your industry. We'll explore later how important demos and customer testimonials are for credibility.

Likeability – Investors aren't just judging your company; they are judging you. They want to discover whether or not you are someone they can work with. It's not being a smiley yes-man or woman; they want to know that you are coachable, they want to know you have a flexible mindset, that you can take guidance without arguing and without an ego flare-up. They aim to help you grow as much as possible, and not just increase your bank account. Remember, you're going to spend many years together, through thick and thin, sickness and health – for better and for worse – they want to know that you will be someone who is a partner. (Sounds a bit like a marriage? Investment periods can last way longer than marriages in this day and age!)

Momentum – People want to invest in winners. You need to show them you aren't floundering around, because they want to join something exciting that's going to new heights. Numbers speak volumes: Growth, revenues, partnerships, pipeline, reviews and testimonials can work well here. This is because they show that people already like what you do and are effusive in their praise.

The key thing is weaving this into your presentation. Make sure each slide reflects at least one of the above points and hits its sweet spot.

This can also inform the question of WHERE to put your Team slide. Beginning? End? Somewhere in the middle? I always tell my clients - if your team adds to your credibility - meaning you have serial entrepreneurs with exits under their belts, former Execs from well known companies, big names on your Advisory Board, etc., definitely put the Team slide at the front. If you just happen to be a nice group of first-time entrepreneurs (not that there's anything wrong with that!), wait till a bit later when you have grabbed their attention in other ways, and then put it towards the end of Act III.

How do you showcase likeability? That doesn't have a slide, does it? I once had a VC tell me they saw so many good companies that they always looked for reasons to say "no" rather than "yes". For example, his biggest pet peeve was if a founder glanced at their phone during a meeting. This was a big no-no and an automatic red flag for them, and a strikeout. Sounds a bit extreme? Maybe – but they see how you behave during the meeting as indicative of how you will behave in your business.

Here are a few big red flags I've heard VCs call out:

Don't Make Excuses – If something doesn't work – screen resolution, sound, etc. – don't go making excuses for it. They might not have noticed until you drew attention to it. One of the startups that presented in a pitch session I was at had a sound technology solution they were hoping to get funding for. Suddenly, when they got to the demo, the sound was barely discernible, playing from their laptop, even at full volume. Nobody could hear the "state of the art" sound from the clip they showed of a stadium they worked with. Needless to say, they were mortified and kept apologizing for the poor sound. I cringed. First of all, it didn't really sound that bad, it was just low, but after they called attention to it, the investors thought it did. Second of all, if you have a sound element – you had better make sure you come with the most advanced portable speakers around! Ditto for a visual-oriented product – high-resolution screen and stellar graphics.

Don't Argue – One of the biggest faux pas I see Founders make is arguing a point with an investor or outright saying that they disagree. You might disagree with them, or you might even have proof that they are wrong. Arguing will get you nowhere and will send them running for the hills because if you argue in your first meeting, how will board meetings look? As hard as it might be, just sit there, accept the feedback magnanimously, and try not to take it as a personal affront. Perhaps follow up later with a note thanking them for their feedback and adding some stats that politely back up your point, or just leave it alone. Better to be smart and funded, than right and penniless.

Take Notes – One of the things VCs look for is the attentiveness of the entrepreneur – you should be taking notes – otherwise, it's a glaring sign that you are not being attentive. The CEO should at least appear to be taking notes, even if the CTO or CMO is also there, scribbling furiously. Pen and paper or notebook look more like note taking than taking notes on your laptop – or worse – your phone! For all they know, you could be checking your email and not listening to them. As one VC partner said, "Until you visibly accept our feedback – i.e. take notes and nod – we don't think you got it. We need that visual cue."

What's in a Why

Every good story has a conflict. Actually, let me rephrase: Every good story includes solving an epic conflict. Think of any memorable movie or series you've watched, a book you've read, or even a viral social media post. They all swivel around, cracking an issue. The same is true for your startup. You wouldn't have come up with it if there wasn't a challenge to overcome, a disruption to fix, or a need to satisfy. The conflict describes WHY you're doing what you're doing. It's not just "the problem" or "the villain", which we will dive into later - it's the greater good, the bigger picture, the ultimate vision which wakes you up every morning and keeps you up late at night.

The WHY is your driver, your fuel, and your incentive – it's the big bang of your story. And that's what investors are looking for when you present to them, not just what you're doing right now, but rather your raison d'etre.

Simon Sinek understood this when he shaped his vision of people not buying what you do but why you do it. In his epic book "Start with the Why," he teaches that it's human nature to want to know the motivation behind an action or an offer. Now, remember that investors are humans too. Every psychological truth applies to them as much as to anyone else.

Investors are also awash in a flood of pitches, containing endless numbers and facts, playing catch in their heads; which figures go with which solution? If you want to make sure that your idea is the one that sticks, you need to create an emotional connection using a story around your WHY.

Let Investors in on the motivation that drove you toward seeking answers. Approach it as if it were a precious secret waiting to be revealed, because when you do, your potential investors already feel part of the solution. Adding value and purpose to your idea creates an emotional point of connection for Investors.

Your WHY is the vision that drives you forward through iteration upon iteration of your product, leading to the coveted "one-day-when-you-have-become" the market leader; that company which has done something profound. It's not necessarily solving world hunger or getting to net zero carbon (although it might be), but it should be a tectonic shift in the way things are done today in your market. It's the combination of being a visionary, execution of the vision, the path forward, and tangible, measurable results proving your need and worth, that makes up the golden ticket to getting funded.

SHOW YOU REALLY CARE.

There's more to it. People and investors want to know you care. Nobody likes to buy from people or invest in businesses whose only motivation is to satisfy their own need for profit. At the very basic level, you need to show you care about the customer. In the case of investors, demonstrate respect for their potential investment. It's simple psychology.

Before anyone gives you funding, they need to believe they are contributing towards a significant change in the market or a betterment of people's lives. They need to be convinced the money they pull out of their pockets will do something valuable other than raise the stack of dollars in your bank account – and theirs, eventually.

This is what Silicon Valley investors call the "North Star." This is your opportunity to give investors the big picture of your company or product, connecting what you do in practice with a bigger cause, vision, or revolution they should care about and see massive potential in. This is still in the opening slide — not even the actual meat of the presentation.

HOW TO BUILD YOUR 'WHY' STATEMENT

There's no one right way to find your 'why' – it's as unique as your DNA – it's in your company's DNA. But here are a few guidelines to build your why statement:

Ask yourself: "Why did I start this journey?"
Ask yourself: "What do you REALLY hope to achieve?"
Ask yourself: "If money and time were not obstacles – what would you really want to do with your company?"

Ask yourself: "What is the seismic shift in the market you will create?"
Ask yourself: Five years from now, when you have been acquired, IPO'd, or had a major funding or liquidity event, and TechCrunch writes about you – what will they call you? The company that did X for Y? (What are your X and WHY? ;))

Let's be clear - this is a moonshot. This is not your product now, rather what it has the potential to become. You need help getting funded to bring you closer to that dream, and eventually, that vision becoming a reality.

Here are a few examples of 'Why' statements of well-known companies – note how they don't mention their products or technology at all:

MICROSOFT
"To enable people and businesses throughout the world to realize their full potential"

AMAZON.COM
"To be Earth's most customer-centric company, where customers can find and discover anything they might want to buy online, and endeavors to offer its customers the lowest possible prices"

LINKEDIN
"To connect the world's professionals to make them more productive and successful"

GOOGLE
"To organize the world's information and make it universally accessible and useful"

FACEBOOK
"To give people the power to share and make the world more open and connected"

INTUIT
"To improve its customers' financial lives so profoundly, they couldn't imagine going back to the old way"

Examples of 'Why' statements of well-known companies

I particularly love Intuit's - that's sheer stickiness. If you can get a client to say they can never imagine going back to life before you -

that's a hugely positive signal for investors.

We will circle back to your 'Why' later in your pitch, where we will have another great place to use it.

So take a beat and ponder - what's your 'Why'? Jot it down and come back when you're ready to move on. It is a great exercise to do with your team as well - see how they see the 'Why'.

THE BRAG SLIDE

It's human nature to want to share great news - Congratulations - you got a new job! Congratulations - you bought a new home! Congratulations - a new baby is on the way!

The glow of all the good wishes and 'likes' from friends is an intrinsic reward in and of itself.

So if you have good news that could significantly increase the odds of you getting funded, why would you not be shouting it from the rooftops?

I've sat through countless pitch decks over the years and seen too many founders focus on how amazing their idea is, rather than how great their execution has been to date. If you've had recent breakthroughs like closing big contracts, an exciting partnership and even a lead investor - don't wait until slide 17 to show it off – some investors might have already lost interest by then!

As one VC partner I spoke to put it: "As investors, we look for exceptional strength in a company – your traction is just that – PUT IT AT THE BEGINNING – we built it – it's working – here's how. In VC land, we say that the best companies will lead with an MRR (Monthly Run Rate) slide."

If there's one thing investors know, it's how difficult it is to close funding, land clients, or forge partnerships. It shows momentum on your part and will completely change the way they listen to the rest of your pitch. It's not empty words or arrogance if it's the truth!

So if you have significant accomplishments, start with a summary up front. Bring in the big numbers sooner, and move logos of paying customers to the front of the presentation; if you have revenue – LEAD WITH IT!!! Even if it's small – it can convert to much more significant numbers. Ultimately you worked hard to get this – so bring it front and center.

If you have these impressive stats, right after your title slide, you should go straight into what I call the "brag slide". The brag slide is all about getting the investor's attention immediately and keeping it throughout your entire pitch. You've got to make a solid first impression, especially in conditions where interest rates could be on the rise and money will be harder to come by.

It's doubly crucial if you've already raised your Series A or beyond. By now, you've had significant capital injections, therefore your results achieved with the funding you've already received need to be spectacular to convince investors to give you even more money.

I know, I know, it's hard to toot your own horn, but the thing is, humility won't get you funded. A brag slide might make you feel uneasy. Some founders I've worked with don't want to seem arrogant by listing out their wins immediately. Yet this isn't about stereotypical vanity metrics but sharing meaningful progress updates which are useful to investors. For instance, investors don't need to know how many followers you have on TikTok unless they are converting to paid customers. I'm suggesting you include your actual accomplishments, the numbers you've worked so hard to achieve - this is your blood, sweat and tears - why shouldn't you brag about it?

"But they don't know what we do yet!" you are shouting at me!

It's okay not to explain the basics of your product first because: Most investors will have done at least some homework on you before the meeting, so they kind of have some idea what it is that you do.

If they haven't, you can instantly wow them and make them curious.

Once you hit them with big numbers, they'll be dying to know, in the following slides, what your underlying business is, to have generated such amazing results.

You should aim for around six to eight killer numbers on the slide that are relevant to your business's financial success. Here are some ideas of what you can use:

Top-line revenue growth - Past growth isn't an indicator of future growth, but you're positively anchoring investor expectations. Show them you know what you're doing. You can use MoM (Month over Month), QoQ (Quarter over Quarter), or YoY (Year over Year), whichever is the most impressive overall. And you can also show user growth - even if it's not all paying yet.

ARR/MRR - (Annual or Monthly Recurring Revenue, or Run Rate) For subscription-based companies, a strong annual or monthly recurring revenue shows stability and stickiness. In particular, tell investors about any long-term deals or deals that have a long lifetime - some enterprise deals are signed for 3-5 years, and that's great because it shows inherent stickiness and predictable revenue.

Intellectual property - Any patents approved or pending show your business has a competitive advantage over others looking to do the same thing.

Big partnerships - When big brands treat you as a trusted partner, you benefit from credibility by association, so use it as leverage.

Pipeline - $17 million worth of contracts poised to be signed in the next year? No investor dislikes a startup with a strong sales pipeline.

Current funding backers - If you've already had commitments from venture capitalists to invest in you this round, then let potential investors know pronto. Investors usually respect the opinions of their peers.

You might look at this list with a sense of dread. Maybe all of those numbers look pretty blah for you right now, and that's understandable because it's a tough economy out there. Businesses in this situation have even more reason to start on a positive note though! In this case - don't feel the need to start with a brag slide. We'll cover what else you can do when we get to the traction slide.

Traction can make Investors a believer. If they don't resonate with your market, but you show them traction to prove its strength – the numbers are a potent persuader. If your solution resonates with many different clients in many industries – that's even better.

Disclaimer - please don't call it a brag slide, that's just our little inside joke, because calling it a "brag slide" could come off a bit, well, braggy. Name it something like "Highlights and Milestones" or " Traction to Date."

Here are a few great examples of Brag Slides from clients of mine:

Armadillo - a Home Warranty platform based in NY, offering affordable, trustworthy coverage for all home maintenance and repair needs - geared for the new age of homeowners. At the time of writing this, they were in the process of raising their Series A. Their numbers are off the charts, and the format is simple and easy to follow:

Notice that they discussed growth in sales (numbers and value), pipeline, partnerships, supply/demand as well as some mega deals (sorry, had to blur those out by request). This is definitely a great way to grab investor attention fast!

Another client of mine, Pashion, has an incredible patented technology for shoes that go from heel to flat in a mere second.

Haley Pavone, their Founder and CEO, shared their brag slide:

As a retail/consumer company, she also stressed repeat business (or stickiness), profit margins and virality; 95% of customers are likely to refer a friend. Honestly, it's a walking virality play (pun intended) because anyone that sees the shoes is instantly going to ask about them and want them!

ACT I - THE PROBLEM (AKA THE VILLAIN)

Here's a harsh revelation. I'm sorry, but:

NOBODY CARES ABOUT YOUR PRODUCT/SOLUTION/TECHNOLOGY - **unless** you can first prove **why** they need it in their lives.

I've met hundreds of companies over the years, working on their sales or fundraising materials and almost every time, they start by telling me about their product/solution/technology, why it's great, why it will change the world. They then proceed to launch into details of the technology. I sit there smiling politely, thinking, "Why should I care???" If I felt this way, imagine what the investors/customers/partners that had to listen to their ramblings were thinking.

THE VILLAIN IS THE HERO OF YOUR STORY

What do Star Wars, Silence of the Lambs, and The Dark Knight have in common?

Yes, they all were massive box office hits. But they also have a larger-than-life villain.

Who can ever forget Darth Vader? Hannibal Lecter or Heath Ledger's haunting version of the Joker?

These villains stay with us for years and send a chill down our spine whenever we see them. In an action-adventure movie, usually in the first few minutes, we meet the villain or see a villainous act they have perpetrated - a murder/kidnapping/bombing etc. This initial encounter keeps us glued to our seats till the very end.

Now, imagine that these villains didn't exist... What would these movies be? Sappy dramas with semi-shallow characters that are nice to look at, but pretty dull.

The villain is actually the hero of these movies. They drive the action, they cause the conflict, and they make the hero or heroine look great.

Different Types of Villains

When talking about the villain, or the problem in your startup pitch, there are two main ways you can go.

People are motivated by two main things:

To avoid something bad happening

To make something good happen

It's the classic carrot vs. the stick. Which one is more powerful? It depends on your audience, and what type of product you're selling. If you're in cyber security, you are likely pushing the "stick" - scaring them a bit about what might happen if they don't do something to protect themselves. If you're a productivity solution, likely it's the carrot, showing how much better their life can be. This is the Advil vs. the vitamin. And don't get me wrong - the vitamin story can be just as lucrative if you play your numbers right.

When pitching your startup, start by hitting them where it hurts - your user's "villain" - what's missing in their lives? What might happen if they don't take measures? What won't they be able to live without, etc? They will be so anxious for a solution that you will be their new "Hero."

A "Villain" exercise for your pitch:

Identify your Audience - Who are you speaking to/selling to/ attempting to persuade? Depending on whether that person is a potential investor, customer, or partner; the villain will look different.

Take a Walk in their Shoes - Ask yourself, what the biggest pain in their life is. Try to feel it, get a sense of it and really empathize with them. With an Investor, it might not be a villain in their life, but rather a villain in your target audience's life that's worth a lot of money if your hero can solve it.

Show them you "Get it" - Find a way to illustrate their villain:
Personal Story - showing that you understand the situation - this works great with investors (i.e. we went on vacation last Summer, and we realized that we had spent over half of our budget on hotel rooms...)

The "As if" Situation - give a story of someone that encountered the problem - either a real or imagined client of yours. (i.e. Jane and John went on vacation last summer. They saved up for over a year to be able to afford it - but the biggest, most unavoidable expense, was the hotel…)

Case Study - complete with persuasive numbers (i.e. did you know that in the US, people spend 65% of their vacation budget on hotels…?)

Try a few different villain stories and test which works best.

In the next section, you will see some of these villain stories come to life as I share with you some founder story examples that really worked.

THE FOUNDER STORY

If you have a story that inspired you to begin this crazy journey as an entrepreneur, this should definitely be your 'villain' story. Suppose the villain you encountered in your own life or the life of someone you care about was so powerful that it made you drop your cushy day job and embark on the roller coaster ride of entrepreneurship. In that case, it's a potent signal to investors that you are genuinely committed to this venture because you have a personal stake. And these stories, as stories do, stick with them and resonate, making them think, "Oh, I get that; I could see myself/spouse/parents using that…" And this is precisely the effect you want to create.

I want to share a few of my favorite Founder stories I've helped tell over the years, to inspire you to tell your own. I will preface this by saying that I have told these stories and retold them again and again over the years to the point where I almost feel I was part of them and can see them unfolding - so I might have some of the details mixed up or inferred - but the beauty of a good story is that it's the heart of it that really matters.

FOUNDER STORY #1 - THE HEALING STORY - CURALIFE

Undoubtedly, any startups in the biomed, pharma, life sciences or the medical device space have a distinct advantage when it comes to storytelling - they deal with the human condition, our health, our bodies, and our lives. Therefore they touch on something deep and emotional in every one of us and I always encourage founders to use this emotional resonance to their advantage.

Imagine, for example, that one of your parents suddenly was diagnosed with a chronic illness. Wouldn't you do everything you can to help them maintain their quality of life as much as possible? Ron Elul, a serial entrepreneur, took this one to new heights.

At the age of 56, Ron's father, Rafi, was diagnosed with type 2 diabetes. He wasn't obese and was in good health. It came as a total shock to all of them, even though there was a family history of diabetes, and it wasn't wholly unexpected. Suddenly, Rafi had to make DRAMATIC lifestyle changes. And for someone who loved to eat, especially his wife's cooking - having the pleasures of life stripped away in an instant was as big a blow as knowing that he'd have to be using oral diabetes drugs and checking his blood sugar every day for the rest of his life.

After nine months on two types of medications, working out, and eating right - his situation had worsened - going from 150 to 300 daily glucose level, not to mention the physical and emotional strain - losing his concentration levels - going from an avid reader to someone who couldn't read for more than 15 minutes, having to constantly use the bathroom, exhaustion, collapsing for an hour nap every day. This all was taking a heavy toll on his emotional state, especially seeing that the treatment wasn't making things any better.

As a family, the Elul's took on a mission of trying to find something, anything, that could help better their beloved father's condition. Ron traveled high and low - from Africa to Serbia - looking for a miracle solution, but nothing was viable. The closest system he found was Ayurveda which was a good base - but still, it wasn't the perfect solution.

(Now we move to tying it to the bigger, industry wide problem):

The Elul family are not alone - there are 425 million people diagnosed with diabetes each year, quadrupling since the 80's - growing at a 7% CAGR (Compound Annual Growth Rate), considered to be the biggest threat of our time - second only to HIV. There are 86 million people diagnosed as pre-diabetic in the US, at high risk of developing type 2 diabetes in the next ten years.

Diabetes is also considered a "gateway disease," causing complications of oxygen flow to the extremities, resulting in over 900,000 amputations of the foot each year, and two-thirds of diabetics, like Rafi, are unable to achieve glucose balance and meet their treatment goals.

$1.1 billion are invested each year in diabetes research, and still, there isn't a solution that strikes a balance between side effects and efficacy.

So Ron decided to take matters into his own hands, taking the basis of Ayurveda - to create the world's best solution for helping diabetics live a balanced, full life. He founded Curalife to develop natural products that significantly improve the quality of life for all chronic patients, starting where his heart was - Diabetes - with their flagship product - Curalin, a natural supplement for type 2 diabetics, helping to lower and stabilize glucose levels quickly and to balance sugar levels in the 'normal' range within a few months.

The results were staggering, and they quickly added additional products and offerings. Rafi is now in much better health and came on to be chairman of Curalife. Great story, right?

You might be asking if you need to have to have a sick family member to tell a good story. No - there are many other stories that can be told.

FOUNDER STORY #2 - THE SOUVLAKI STORY - EATWITH

This is, without a doubt, one of my all-time favorite Founder stories! I met the EatWith founders, Guy and Shemer, back in 2011 when I was mentoring pitches at a startup accelerator. I instantly loved their idea - but I felt there was a story behind it that would make it shine even more. So I asked where the idea came from. Guy's eyes lit up (this is a common side effect of talking about your origin story - your passion and excitement shine through, which has a powerful impact on investors because it shows your true connection and drive!) and he told me this story:

"It was on our honeymoon! We were in the Greek Islands searching for authentic, local food, the kind that you dream about for years to come. And we looked and looked and looked, but all we could see for miles around was souvlaki, souvlaki, souvlaki. And it was featured on those tacky blue touristy signs with faded, unappetizing pictures. This was NOT what we had in mind.

Finally, in a moment of desperation, I stopped a local woman who was walking home with baskets of produce from the market, and I asked: "Excuse me, can you tell me where the locals eat?" She looked perplexed by the question, but she said, "What do you mean, where do we eat? We eat at home!" Half-jokingly I said, "Well, how do I get a reservation?" Again, she looked a bit flummoxed, but without missing a beat, she said, "Oh, you want to come for dinner?" My wife and I were embarrassed and turned the color of the tomatoes peeking out of her basket. I tried to explain that I was joking and she said "No, no! You should come!"

Sheepishly I took down her address and agreed to be there at eight that night. We had no idea what to expect and thought of not showing up, but I was too intrigued. When we arrived at her modest-looking home, we were amazed at what we saw - a table set for a group of 10, with glistening salads, juicy fish, crusty bread, and local cheeses - it was a site for sore souvlaki eyes!

Not only was the meal sumptuous, but the conversation was also scintillating. We were there with locals and other tourists and learned much about the island's life. It was a magical night full of great food and endless Ouzo. I thought - 'this is the way EVERYONE should experience travel! Like a local!' And EatWith was born.

EatWith is like an Airbnb for meals - where you could book an experience with a local home - anywhere from your hometown to an exotic vacation destination, and have a meal with a local family, immersing yourself, if only for an evening, in a slice of local life, flavors and customs. In 2017 EatWith was acquired by the European company Vizeat, which is still active, and you can experience an EatWith experience in many places around the world.

Granted, I heard this story about 11 years ago, yet I have told it again and again at pitching workshops because it's a great example of simple, yet masterful storytelling, and it is still as alive to me as the day I heard it. I can see the little old woman (at least in my mind she's old!), the cobblestones, and the table laden with delicious dishes. I'm sure I have embellished and altered Guy's telling of the story - but the power of storytelling is that it lives on with you; it becomes public domain to tell and retell, drawing people in, making them drool over the table they imagine, reminding them of the time they were stuck with local tourist traps and longed for an authentic experience, or the time they found that hole-in-the-wall gem of a restaurant that became the highlight of their trip. Does it matter if I told the story verbatim or not? No. Will you remember this story after reading it? If you love food and travel as much as I do - it's quite likely!

FOUNDER STORY #3 - THE TOKYO STORY

I would love to tell you who this company is, but I have been asked to keep it anonymous, so I will respect that.

Several years ago, I met with a very technical team. I mean, VERY technical. Every other word was "computer vision," "AI," "deep learning," "machine learning," "image analysis," etc. They rattled on for a while, and I was left in a daze. After listening for ten minutes, I had absolutely no clue what they did!

I started trying to peel away layers of the onion to get to the core of the story. Finally, one of the team members said - "Look, this one time when we were in Tokyo…" I felt my storytelling antennae perk up and I said, "Wait, wait - you mean you came up with this idea in Tokyo??? Why didn't you say so?." And they rolled their eyes and continued to say that they came from a background of computer vision and deep learning, blah blah blah… This time I stopped them, and I said: "Ok, listen up - you all came up with this idea in Tokyo - Capish?" They looked at me as if I had just landed from Mars - but after a few minutes - they got it. Because doesn't it sound sexier to say something like:

"We were roaming the streets of Tokyo feeling 'Lost in Translation' (Badum bum…). We were dazzled by the gorgeous buildings - yet had absolutely no clue what we were looking at! And one of us said, 'wouldn't it be cool if we could just snap a pic and instantly our phone would tell us what we were looking at, the history of the building, what was around - maybe a cool place nearby to have drinks?' And then we thought - 'well, with our extensive background in AI, computer vision and image analysis - why couldn't we build a product like that?' and a start-up was born."

Now, did a single investor ask to see their passport to check what date they had been in Tokyo and what date they incorporated? I assure you, not one. Does it really matter if that was the exact moment they came up with the idea or if it was at an early seedling stage and perhaps later, on a trip to Tokyo, they got validation? It doesn't matter.

What matters is that every investor in the meeting was doing what you are likely doing now - thinking of a time when you traveled to a country where you were unfamiliar with the language. How lost and overwhelmed did you feel? How much would you have paid to have a 'tour guide in your pocket?' The company raised tens of millions and went on to become an AR/VR solution embedded in car windshields as well (think pop-up video as you drive).

The power of storytelling is that it is so human, so much at the core of our experience, that we continuously look for ways to connect to other peoples' stories. And when we do, we "get" them on a much deeper level than we do with techno-babble. These are the true moments of human connection that create the relationships we strive for, with investors, customers or with any other human.

THE DECONSTRUCTED USER STORY

Not everyone has a powerful, colorful origin story to tell. There are other means of captivating your audience with storytelling. One of those methods is another favorite of mine, which I call the "Deconstructed User Story." Suppose you already have customers (hopefully paying customers). In that case, you can increase your credibility and momentum even more by using their story to illustrate the problem you are solving, and then later, you can then use them to show off the solution. Hence why I call this deconstructed. The story is split into yin and yang, or before and after.

I'll share the deconstructed user story of one of my clients, who again I will leave anonymous since they deal with very sensitive cyber attacks, namely Ransomware. This happens when a hacker takes control of a computer - or an entire network and blocks access to it until they are paid an exorbitant ransom, usually in Bitcoin, so it can't be traced.

When the Founders came to our session, they were also highly technical and very hard to understand. So, as usual, I rolled up my sleeves and went digging for a story. I asked them which of their many paying clients had a great success story we could use. Here's the story we put together:

"A US hospital chain with 400 facilities was under a Ransomware attack. Imagine, every medical facility in the chain blocked, with no access to patient records, highly sensitive information in danger of being compromised, and even HVAC and medical devices no longer able to be used because the systems were managed digitally.

It took them three weeks to get back up and running, with revenue losses of ~$30 million per day - a total of $665 million in operational losses, not to mention the undisclosed ransom payout. But the real collateral damage was reputation. And even scarier, IBM published a study showing that an organization that has been hacked once has an increased likelihood of being hacked again within 12-18 months.

The most astounding part was that the organization discovered that the attackers were lurking in the system for months before the attack happened, giving them a foothold on 50-60% of the system. They exfiltrated sensitive data - so if the ransom wasn't paid - not only were the systems held hostage - but the sensitive data would have been leaked."

(And now comes the part where we tie the specific user story to the broader problem and bring in some impressive numbers, stats and quotes from industry leaders, proving that this is a massive problem with no viable solution until now):

"We've seen these attacks across all industries - from semiconductors to financial institutions to government agencies. The problem has escalated dramatically with the majority of workforces in tech companies working from home, with VPN and endpoint security becoming far more complex to manage, and with far more vulnerable points for penetration.

Interpol shows there has been a rise in cyber threats driven by COVID - and even after the pandemic - over 65% of all tech companies have made work from home a permanent policy - Mark Zuckerberg predicted that up to half of Meta's employees would work from home within five to ten years.

If there's one common thread between ALL major cyber attacks in the past three years - it's "Evasive Malware" - malware that goes undetected for months, and, in the meantime, does its dirty deed - and once it's detected - it's too late to prevent the damage.

With sooooo many cyber solutions out there - how is this still happening? (This is very important because it addresses a burning question that an investor is likely asking - "what makes you different from all the hundreds of other cyber solutions I see come across my desk?")

Well, the problem is, most of the cyber solutions out there are like a smoke detector - the minute there's smoke, the alarm is set off, and we know a fire must be put out.

But what if the arsonist is lurking on site, quietly putting flammable materials in the room, undetected for months? Once the fire is set off - it's too late to prevent the damage. An average attack takes 260 days to detect.

(Now, the segue into the new possibilities and hope that they bring):

But what if we did it differently? What if we created a room with no oxygen - where a fire couldn't even be started? What if we changed the environment with smoke and mirrors so the malware couldn't be malicious? This is precisely what Company X is doing"

Drop mic.

What did we do here?

Illustrated a complex problem by telling a story that's easy to grasp and understand

Built the suspense and showed that this was a growing problem in the industry

Increased their credibility by using a real-life example

Brought in actual stats, numbers, and a Zuckerberg quote

Even used a metaphor of the "fire" and the "oxygen" to explain the philosophy of what they do, which is another powerful storytelling tool

Addressed early on why they were different from other solutions out there

Masterful storytelling!

Later, I'll show you how to write the solution statement and the second half of the deconstructed user story.

Big Headlines, Big Numbers or "A Day in the Life."

While I love having a personal story to tell, or even an actual client story to deconstruct and tell - not everyone has these stories - yet.

Here are additional techniques you can use to storytell the "villain," or pain of your pitch:

Big Headlines

Things that are in the headlines and the talk of the town:

Yahoo. Target. Equifax. Sonic: All Category 5 data breaches. Is your information safe anymore? *(Washington Post headline)* - If you are a cyber security company, showing that breaches happen even to big companies with robust cyber protection is an excellent way to show why current solutions aren't enough. You can also show why what you're doing is different, better, and groundbreaking.

Biden signs the $1 trillion bipartisan infrastructure bill into law *(NPR headline)* - If you have a solution to detecting and repairing infrastructural damage - showing that the President of the United States has made this a top priority is a great motivator.

Protecting Lives and Livelihoods—Concerns as States Reopen *(Bloomberg Law headline)* - As countries, states and cities started to open back up after the long lockdown, there were requirements to put safeguards in place to do so safely - if you're a startup that does contact tracing, instant facial matching to vaccination records, access technologies, etc. - this was good news for the world - and, of course, for you.

BIG NUMBERS

Numbers are a surefire way of grabbing their attention

$300 billion - the value of the equine market. $140 billion - the value of the cybersecurity market - yes - the annual spend on horses is higher than on cyber security solutions - yet there's no technology that can automatically track a horse's health and wellness. (True story! I worked with this company in 2018!)

2.7 million - Registered Nurse (RN) jobs unfilled. In 2019, there were 3 million RNs. This means about half a million of them aren't working as an RN by choice, mainly because of long, inflexible hours. This is driven by the millennial/gig economy mindset, stress, and even though the pay wasn't the top complaint, the way it's managed made it even more frustrating for them - rendering it a profession they simply didn't want. (This company had the solution to give them better flexibility, terms and compensation.)

33 gigatons - of carbon emissions each year - and over 359 gigatons of plastic are manufactured yearly. Plastic accounts for over 5% of all CO_2 emissions. The problem is, plastic is not going anywhere. There has yet to be a solution that is as strong, cost-effective and simple for so many industries - until now... (A company using a new plant-based material to create plastics and construction materials.)

A Day in the Life

Often, investors aren't that familiar with the industry you play in - whether it's an emerging technology - like Web3 or Generative AI, a very technical space - like Devops or Kubernetes, or an area they haven't delved into - like manufacturing floor safety.

In a case like this - you can guide them along an "as if" or a "day in the life" story based on a company or a few companies' stories brought together.

A client of mine has a solution for safety monitoring and

detection on production floors of large manufacturing plants. So we took a series of images from the floor and told this story:

"Before we talk about our technology, I want to give you a glimpse into a day on a factory floor - forget a day - let's look at a window of less than an hour!!!

See this image? (she shows an image from a typical manufacturing workfloor) Lots of people, lots of equipment, lots of inventory - and A LOT of moving pieces

See this red alert here? That vehicle is within too close a contact range with a human worker - potentially taking one of his legs off.

See this? These workers walked in without proper protective gear and helmets.

See this? This worker was on a very sharp cutting machine and got a phone call from his manager. While talking on the phone, he left the device on - and in one moment of distraction, could lose a hand.

See this? A robotic arm whose function is to speed automation. It has a fence around it to keep people at a distance since it moves SO fast and can be dangerous - but workers are clever and find creative ways around it. This guy is WAY too close to the robot, and it could potentially knock him unconscious.

I could go on and on - but you get the point.

Looking at these images after the fact - after all, hindsight is 20/20 - you can see that, unfortunately, it can be just too late. These things need to be spotted much sooner."

Whether these stories were told about a real client or just an amalgamation of cases at different factories doesn't matter. In two minutes, the investors are initiated into the world of production floor safety hazards that cause 2.7 million nonfatal workplace injuries a year, and costs $268 billion to US employers. Cause/effect/cost. Compelling story.

DON'T SPEND TOO LONG WITH THE VILLAIN

Now that we have examined the villain from nearly every possible angle, here's a caveat: It's essential to know the problem you're solving or the opportunity that you're grabbing, but don't spend too long focusing on the problem. As soon as you see that they get it, go straight to why you're solving it more effectively, how much traction you have, etc. Present the case for why it's needed and spend more time on the product and how it works.

If you are speaking to tech-savvy investors (and in Silicon Valley, you likely are), you must elevate how you talk about the problem –

they still want to get it; they just want you to convey it in a sophisticated manner.

Transitioning From the Problem to the Solution

How do we move from Act I to Act II? How do we move from - we have a scary villain - we need a hero! (Cue Bonnie Tyler, 80's children, sing along!).

You can simply move straight into the solution section, or you can make the transition a bit smoother.

You might want a slide that alludes to the fact that current solutions don't cut it - they're partial, siloed, expensive, complex, and not scalable - you choose the correct answer. This is not a competitive landscape slide but rather, a way to answer the question that is screaming in the investor's head: "Yeah, but what about Company X or Company Y? They're already solving it!" Without bad-mouthing your competition or getting too deep into the weeds, you want to show them that those solutions have made significant progress. Show them that your competitors' solutions are either non-optimal, too expensive, too hard to implement, partial at best, or cause a whole slew of additional problems that will need solving.

If you don't want to do an entire slide on this, you can simply put a 'bottom line' at the foot of your slide, giving the summary of the problem and the transition to the solution. Something to the tune of "In the digital transformation era, better, simpler tools are needed - welcome to the era of _____ (Insert your company name)."

You are summarizing the villain, giving them hope of deliverance, and you are ready now to move on to the meat and potatoes (or tofu and lentils?) part of your pitch - your solution, your hero.

ACT II - THE SOLUTION (AKA THE HERO)

By now you should have a pretty clear picture of who your Villain is, why they are a threat and what the "cost" they create is. Now it's time to delve into the world of your "Hero" - otherwise known as The Solution.

Before working with a team, I rarely see a deck that clearly shows what they do. More often than not, the slide that starts the discussion about the solution launches into a broad description of features, what it does, and how it works.

Remember Simon Sinek's Why? Well, Simon highlights three levels of messaging, which he dubs "The Golden Circle":

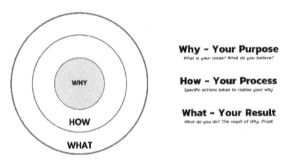

Simon Sinek's Golden Circle

We already covered the 'Why'; now, let's move on to the 'What'. In investor pitching, I approach the 'What' before the 'How'. Until the audience has a true grasp on WHAT you are doing, there's no point launching into a description of HOW it is done.

So how do we describe our solution so simply that an eight-year-old, and even your grandparents would understand?

THE SIMPLE SOLUTION STATEMENT

The Simple Solution Statement will be one of the simplest pieces of text you will write, but it isn't easy to write it! You want to be able to explain your solution in approximately one sentence or statement.

My formula is: "We do X for Y by Z." That's the template. You can play with it and move it around, but that's the main structure. Let's break it down:

"We are an X (tool/solution/platform/app/system) that does Y (solves a specific problem for a particular audience) by Z (how are you doing it? And this doesn't mean going into technical details, but rather the result, product, unique technological approach, secret sauce). If you can crack this code - you will be set.

Here are a few sample solution statements for well-known companies: (Disclaimer - I've totally made these up, they are not their official solution statements.)

Slack - a communication platform (X) that lets teams communicate and collaborate with ease from anywhere, (Y) using a simple, intuitive chat interface (Z).

Airbnb - a site (X) that connects travelers with property owners to help them find affordable lodging 'like locals' while owners make extra income (Y&Z).

Uber - an app (X) that lets anyone order a ride based on their location,(Y) offering an affordable alternative to taxis that's trackable, shareable, and payable with one click (Z).

Medium - a platform (X) that lets anyone become a published writer, (Y) with a simple interface and shareable function, increasing exposure to people interested in what you write, monetizing your efforts (Z).

Now it's your turn - go ahead! Give it a go with your company's simple solution statement. This will probably take many tries, but you'll get it!

MESSAGES FOR GRANDMA

Many moons ago I was giving a presentation skills training for hardware engineers that worked at a large semiconductor company.

These are the toughest nuts to crack because they are HIGHLY technological and struggle to see how anyone else doesn't get what they get.

Case in point, one guy (let's call him Marvin) got up to present, and this is what his opening slide looked like:

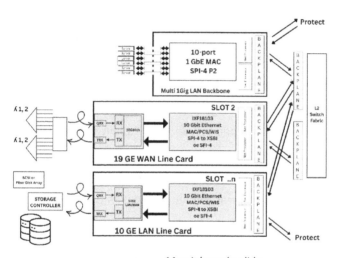

Marvin's geeky slide

Now, not coming from a technical background, and relatively new in my career, I had NO CLUE what he was showing here. I scanned the room to see if his colleagues were enraptured, and whether I had simply missed the most awe-inspiring message ever - but everyone was in various stages of disengagement. Some were doodling, and some were checking emails on their laptop (this was a pre-smartphone era; otherwise, I'm sure they would have been glued to their social feed); others were simply staring blindly into space - I could almost hear them willing the time to move faster.

To add insult to industry, Marvin stood there literally reading EVERY data point on the slide verbatim ad nauseam. I politely let him drone on for a few minutes, which seemed like an eternity and then with all the gentility I could muster, I said, "Thanks, that was interesting (NOT). Now, can you please tell us what it means?"

Marvin looked at me confused, blinked a few times, scratched his head and said. "Um, well, what it means is…" and proceeded to go through the exact verbatim description, only much, much slower, as if he were speaking to a very young child. Again, I stopped him and said: "Okay, let's try this again. Can you explain it to me so my grandmother can understand?" Marvin looked at me, this time incredulously, jaw gaping and said: "You mean your grandmother is an engineer?" (I'm sure he was thinking, "Did it skip a generation or something?")

Poor Marvin, I had to break his geeky heart and tell him that neither of my grandmothers' (rest their souls) had been engineers.

Pause the Marvin story for a second - are your grandparents' engineers? Are your parents'? Do they come from the field that your technology is in? If not, those must be some awkward dinner conversations. Does that mean that they aren't intelligent people? Of course not! Your family are just from different generations, moving in different worlds, and are likely clueless about what you're doing and why it matters. Is that their fault? No. Would you get all haughty and insulting to them about it? I hope not! Because it's your responsibility to ensure they understand it.

You see, it's not about DUMBING the message down, it's about ELEVATING your audience, making them feel smart. When you make people feel smart, they want to be around you, work with you, invest in you. If you make them feel dumb, they just want to disengage.

And believe it or not, Investors want to feel smart too. And they are usually very smart indeed. However, sometimes your technology is complex, nascent, or geared for a particular set of people like developers, system engineers or CISOs, and they too need the message to be simplified.

Case in point, I was coaching pitches for a very prestigious Silicon Valley conference that happened each year (up until the pandemic hit). Part of the conference was a highly sought-after pitch competition, where startups from around the globe were selected to give a five-minute pitch to revolving panels of venture partners from top-tier firms.

I spent a good month before the event conducting pitch sessions with these startups. One of the companies was working on something so complex that I was struggling to crack it. I finally got what they were saying and suggested that they start with a primer, a sort of intro slide to their technology, just in case anyone else in the room was not familiar with it. The CEO scoffed and said, "if an investor doesn't get what we're doing, we don't want them as an investor." "Alrighty then," said I, thinking to myself that they would not get far with that attitude.

Lo and behold, on the day of the event, they got up on stage having made zero adjustments to their pitch. I watched like you watch a car crash about to happen. After the CEO presented, he had three minutes of Q&A with the panel. What do you think the first question was? Yep, one of the VCs asked him, "could you explain that to us in layman's terms?" Honestly, I was surprised at his candor that the VCs had understood nothing. I likely would have simply disengaged and moved on. But this VC voiced what pretty much everyone in the room was thinking: "What the what...?"

It is more important to be smart than right. It's not about you; it's about your audience - whether they are investors, potential partners, customers, or, well, your grandmother. It's about them getting it, understanding it, seeing its value, and moving forward with you. It is not about being blown away by your dubiously impressive knowledge of high-level jargon and incomprehensible terminology.

Albert Einstein said: "If you can't explain it simply, you don't understand it well enough." Though you might argue with him, he was so right! Therefore, you MUST find a way to bring us into your world and explain it simply, in a manner that is matched to the audience you are speaking with. Here are a few guidelines:

Ideas everyone gets - Avoid catchphrases, terminology, or long words that only you or your peers understand. It has to be so clear that even your grandmother, your eight-year-old nephew, even someone from a completely non-technical background would understand. It's our responsibility to make sure we explain it in a way that everyone understands. Break it down into chunks and don't feel the need to explain every bit of the technology - there will be time to dive deeper as they move forward.

Crisp, simple language - We often think big words and professional jargon give us more credibility. The opposite is true - if someone in the audience doesn't understand us, they will feel dumb and disconnected. Even if you have a room of technical experts, they get bored too, so keep your language simple.

Tech 101 - Don't be afraid to have a primer slide. You can always take a moment at the beginning of your presentation to ask, "How familiar are you with this type of technology?" If they say "not very", then have a simple primer slide ready to set the stage for your presentation. If they say "very," then great! Skip the primer slide. Either way, you are ensuring that the understanding is there, without under or overestimating their scope of knowledge.

A Day in the Life - If you are solving a problem for a particular audience, someone with whom we wouldn't be familiar, open up a window into their world and take the Investors on a little journey. (Like we discussed in the villain/problem section). Walk the Investors through your customer's day and the most significant frustrations they have in their lives - and as you go, you can name the terminology for these struggles - that way, when you get to the solution, it's easy for us to refer back to.

Talk it through - It's okay if you are struggling with this - it's tough when you're doing it yourself. I get it. It takes time and practice. The best thing to do is sit down with someone, not from your field, and talk it over with them until they get it. See what questions they ask and answer them, distilling the answers repeatedly until you have a clear way that they understand. This is what storytellers like me are good at - so feel free to reach out to one, or me :).

Oh and what about Marvin? Well, we talked the idea back and forth and finally, I got it. All that he was REALLY trying to say was, "Grandma, we're doing much more in much less space! You know Grandma, once upon a time, computers were so big and bulky that they took up ENTIRE rooms. Today - your smartphone is a bazillion times smaller and a bazillion times faster. How cool is it that they managed to get so much power into something so small? Well, that's exactly what our team is working on! It reminds me of your kitchen, Grandma. It's tiny, yet you churn out food for an army! How do you do it, Grandma?"

We broke it down to something simple, gave an example of a past product and then an analogy to something from her world. (Um, he didn't say bazillion, that's me lol). I hope Marvin ended up having this little talk with his grandma, and I hope she was as proud of Marvin as I was at that moment!

You are NOT Uber for X...

When meeting a startup for the first time, I often ask them what they do. They will say something like: "We're a [insert popular company name] for [insert target audience]. AKA, we're 'Uber for X.'" It always makes me think of a funny site called itsthisforthat.com, which creates an answer to the question: "So what does your startup do?" After hitting refresh, it generates a statement starting with "So, basically, it's like a …". Here are some of the random answers when I had a go:

SO, BASICALLY, IT'S LIKE A:
'Pinterest for Tech Incubators'
'Dollar Shave Club for your cat's litter box'
'Product hunt for hunters'
'Tinder for Fast-Casual Restaurants'
And the list goes on and on…

Why do we feel the need to explain ourselves using another company? Is it because we think it will bring instant recognition? Or will the cache of that company rub off on us? Adam Grant, an organizational psychologist at Wharton School of Business says:

"To generate creative ideas, it's important to start from an unusual place. But to explain those ideas, they have to be connected to something familiar. That's why so many startups are introducing themselves as the 'Uber for X.'"

On the one hand, explaining what you do based on a well-known product puts things in an immediate context, and I've had investors tell me that they really appreciate the quick reference. The problem is, it can pigeonhole you. It automatically seems like you are trying to compete with them even if you're not, and it can confuse matters even more. It also might make you look like a feature or a subset of the company you're comparing to.

I've seen many investors roll their eyes when told that a startup is Uber for X; however, I understand the need to try to cling to something familiar. What's a better way?

In his timeless article on Series B decks, Reid Hoffman recommends using analogies. Still, he cautions about reasoning by analogy: "In startup land, you're running across a minefield, so the details matter, and you have to be careful with your analogies as you conceive strategy. In fact, when I'm the investor listening to a pitch, one detail I consider is whether the entrepreneur is being too deluded by their analogies and not thinking hard enough about exception cases."

Are there any cases where it should be used? Hoffman continues by saying that if you can leverage another company's success to prove that you will be as successful as well, go for it!: "When pitching by analogy, anchor your business to other valuable businesses to signal that your business will be valuable, too."

So if you really are an Airbnb for government officials, go ahead and use the comparison, by all means.

Hoffman concludes that many investors are fatigued hearing the analogy argument and cautions not to force it - "It's better to have no analogy than a bad one."

What should you do instead? Go back to the "Simple Solution Statement" section and keep working on the "We do X for Y by Z" angle. Explaining your solution in one stand-alone sentence is challenging but so important - and so useful for pitching, networking, and simply explaining what you do to people. If you do it simply, concisely, and powerfully – there's no need to compare yourself to this - or that.

THE DEMO, THE HOW, THE STAR OF THE SHOW

The lights go down at a major tech competition and electricity crackles in the air. People actually set down their phones for a rare moment to listen to the ten most promising startups du jour. The first

CEO gets up and starts presenting in the polished manner we'd been working so hard on. He flips the screen to begin his live demo and -

"No internet connection" appears on the blank screen.

He looks mortified. The IT team starts to scramble, the audience murmurs and gets back on their phones, and I bury my face in my hands. Three and a half minutes later, which felt like an eternity, he was up and running again - but the momentum was lost...

Only one hour before it had all worked perfectly at the final tech run-through - so what went wrong? Who knows - and unfortunately, who cares? By that time, he was a distant memory, and despite having REALLY great technology, he did not win the competition, through no fault of his own.

Let's get something straight - you must have a demo! You've shown the 'Why', and the 'What'. The Demo is your 'How' - how it works, how they will use it. It closes Simon Sinek's golden circles.

Now that we've cleared that up, here's a fact: LIVE DEMOS DIE! (often). I have seen it happen too many painful times. I've seen some great saves, like a Founder continuing without missing a beat when the screen wouldn't flip to his Reflector app, and he stood there waving his Smartphone at the audience showing the app. Unfortunately, it was too far to really see, but kudos to him for trying. At least he kept them engaged.

And it's not just at conferences/demo days/competitions - it happens at investor meetings too, like the founder with the sound-enhancing technology we talked about earlier, whose audio didn't sound too great and reflected badly on him and his product. Needless to say, he showed up at the next meeting with a pair of state-of-the-art **wired** speakers to avoid any technical pitfalls.

Your demo should take them through the customer journey – who is your target customer base? What are your current customers telling you – where are they hurting, and why are they using your solution? Give specific examples of how they use it. You don't need a live demo – talk through the customer experience. Define the inflection point people reach, showing that this is the right time for your product.

It is super important to be able to showcase your product visually. Human beings are very visual creatures, and investors, panelists or audience members need to see (or hear) what you're talking about. But not at the cost of fumbling and bumbling.

So how do you create a great Demo that looks and feels (almost) live?

Take a Piece of Your Product Video - If you've already invested in a product video (Which shouldn't be more than 60 seconds), take the part that shows the demo of your product - 20-30 seconds and instead of the voice-over talking, you can talk it through live.

DIY Demo - If you don't yet have the resources to invest in a product video, you can create a product demo by capturing your screen. A popular, free, and relatively easy-to-use tool is Camtasia or on a Mac Screenflow or iMovies. If you have an app, you can use a reflector app to stream onto your screen - but don't do this live; pre-record it. You can try simply casting to a screen live, but as we've seen, it's very risky.

A Semi-Live Demo - During the same competition with the big tech fail, one of the other founders recorded a user session of their product and then played it as if she was using it on the spot. It looked flawless, and nobody knew this was a pre-recorded demo - it looked totally live, but she had safeguarded it to ensure it would work. Powerful and resourceful.

Screenshots/Mock-ups - Put together a series of screenshots, mockups, or wireframes of your product to illustrate the story. That way, you can highlight the features you discuss and give them visual cues. Make sure they look good, though! Shoddy screenshots=shoddy product in the investors' eyes.

Tell a Story - Remember a day in the life and the deconstructed user story from the villain section? Let your demo be the story of the first-time user experience. Use a real customer story, an imagined one or just an overriding narrative that guides them through the user journey. This helps them visualize how easy and cool it is to use your product. You want them to think about themselves or someone they know using it.

Steal the Show - I've seen it all - from human bar charts to mini-Land

Rovers on stage, light-up toilets, bikers and a Broadway-worthy musical demo. Yes, all of the above were demo day or pitch competition demos, and if you ask anyone which start-up they remembered, what do you think the answer is? So get creative - be irreverent but be memorable! However, leave this for the stage. In an investor meeting, being that irreverent runs the risk of not seeming serious enough and losing their trust.

Remember - your demo is the first impression they have of your product - make it a good one!

Features and Benefits - Avoid "Feature Fatigue"

Sometimes I've sat through a pitch or presentation and heard an endless list of features. After about three, I find my mind wandering and my attention span waning.

I realize it's kind of like pictures of kids - if someone asked me about Lily when she was a newborn, I would excitedly pull out my phone and start flipping through photo after photo. After a while, I realized that people might be smiling politely, but they were over it. I realized the error of my ways and instead started showing 1-3 amazing pictures, getting the "Oh, she's soooo cute!" and I then moved on to talk about them. Some people asked to see more pics, but that was because they wanted to see more, not because I was force-feeding them my entire camera roll.

Investors don't care about your "baby." Really, they don't. Sorry but it's true. However, nobody puts Baby in a corner, so let's focus on what they do care about, which is, "is your baby cool", and will they make lots of money investing in your 'baby'?

So instead of rattling off a list of features, try this:

Choose 3-4 "Wow Features" - Pick the features that will knock their socks off. I know they are all amazing, but leave them wanting more.

Show and Tell - As you walk them through the features, show them in a demo - as detailed in the demo section. This brings the features to life with a visual aspect - and you get to show off how cool your 'baby' looks too!

In Action - If you show the features in the context of the user journey, where your user is actually using the product, it also enhances the veracity because you have a bonafide (hopefully) paying user that uses your product!

The Benefit of Benefits - You can show the key benefits to your end user and/or to multiple stakeholders. Remember to show how it benefits the party who is the PAYING customer, which is not always the end user. Sometimes it's the B2B2B (business to business to business - where you're selling to a business that sells your solution to other businesses). It could also be the B2B2C (business to business to consumer - where you sell to businesses, and they sell to end users or customers.) Some benefits might be shared - you want to have about six to eight - BIG things, like cost savings, productivity, security, efficiency, etc.

Real Results - If you are using a real user story, you can bring in ACTUAL results like: In just three months - 57% growth in revenues, 10x faster checkout process, 67% decrease in cart abandonment, 87% increase in stickiness - anything that shows how you truly brought value to your customer—the more tangible and measurable, the better. And if you don't have real results yet, you can make a conservative projection.

Loving Testimonial - If your customer is blown away and loves you, get it in writing! We'll talk more about it in the next section.

And please, if you see them losing attention, hemming and hawing or immersed in their smartphones, end the list and move on - you might be showing off 'baby' a little too much :)

Testimonials - Share the Love

I want to tell you a little secret. I close clients before we even get on a call together. Why? This is because my previous clients do all the work for me. I am relentless about asking for testimonials - both video and LinkedIn. It's time-consuming, but it's worth it. And if a new lead hasn't seen the testimonials already, I send them a follow-up email after our intro call with a link to my LinkedIn. There, they will see several hundred testimonials. I also invite them to reach out to anyone on the list and ask to hear more. And I have had prospective clients do just that, check out my "referrals."

You can tell someone how great you are or how great your solution is - but when it comes from someone else, someone similar to them, or an actual, paying user, it will be 100x more potent. However, with all good intentions, people don't usually think about writing a testimonial unless you ask them to. And even after they say yes, they get busy and life gets in the way and they might forget to. (Shocking! You're not the only thing on their mind!) You must follow up and nudge without being too annoying about it. After three attempts, I usually call it a day - and you'd be surprised at how many do it on the third reminder!

For B2B companies, the more respected the source of the review, the better. Let's say you had five customers last year, but only one lasted the entire year. If this customer happens to be Slack and they love working with you, then investors don't need to know much more.

A quote from a valued customer which says they love you, they can't imagine life before you, and they'll never stop using you, demonstrates product market fit and stickiness. You're proving your product solves a pain point in the real world, not just in theory. This can make a huge difference to how investors perceive your product.

So, how do you get, gather, and use testimonials?

Find your champions - Look at a company that uses your technology and find the person or people there that absolutely adore you, can't say enough superlatives, and thank you profusely for making their lives better. When they express their praise, say, "Wow! That's so amazing to hear! Would you mind if I quote you on that?" Sometimes they need to clear it with their legal department; other times, they don't feel comfortable having the name of the company or their own name up there; in that case, you can anonymize it. Often, if you tell them it's for an internal investor presentation and won't be on your website or sales materials, that will make it okay for them to have their name or company used. If they are legally allowed to, most likely, they will instantly agree or get permission to share the quote.

Make it easy on them - If a champion wants to help but doesn't get around to it - offer to write the testimonial for them, and get them to sign off on it - or make some tweaks. It's not easy to write about yourself, but you can gather things they've said or written in emails and pull it together.

Record and display it - Video, written, LinkedIn - anywhere and everywhere you can get them to display the testimonials. And once you have them, ask permission to put it on your website, sales materials and/or investor deck.

Categorize and prioritize - Use different testimonials for different audiences - for investors, choose the testimonials that showcase profuse customer love and stickiness. For potential customers, use testimonials from similar companies in the same industry, but preferably not direct competitors, unless FOMO can egg them on.

Don't just expect that people who love you will share the love; encourage it, capture it and share the love yourself!

Act III - The Biz (aka the Hero's Action Plan)

By this point, hopefully, you have captivated them with your charm, your story, your passion, and a kick-butt product. They're excited, they're into it - but remember - they are investors after all… They're not just in it for the passion and allure - they need to see numbers that prove that, not only are you a great investment opportunity, but you are also a lucrative one that will bring them a 10x return or more.

Act III is where the magic happens. In storytelling terms, you've introduced the villain and explained how the hero will overcome the obstacles. Now you're about to show the hero's journey. What happens after the hero takes action? Act III is about the business, or, your hero's action plan. Each section here can, and should be, its own slide (often, more than one).

Traction - Where the Rubber Meets the Road.

Remember what we discussed earlier about the three things investors really listen for? Credibility, likeability and…

Momentum: the actual, factual difference between a great idea and great execution. This is the place to showcase your achievements, whatever stage you're at. If you did a brag slide, as we discussed earlier, you could get a bit more granular with the big numbers here. If your traction isn't yet brag-worthy, then this is the place to let them know where you are in the process.

Depending on your business model, relevant traction for your business isn't necessarily just going to depend on raw sales numbers. The number of downloads or daily active users can be far more telling for an app or software tool. The number of returning users and repeat business can be powerful indicators of your stickiness and the quality of your products or services.

Your ability to demonstrate some type of traction is key for any investor. You should be able to provide quantifiable data that proves that your company is headed in the right direction. Such statistics help illustrate your brand's growth and appeal to your target market. Investors want to see these numbers growing, not remaining stagnant.

They say the proof is in the pudding – you've got one heck of a pudding to cook here. You must be very convincing on the "What makes you better/different?" question. Everyone today says things like - AI or machine learning makes them better – but that is not an answer; you need to show clear differentiation and have the proof to back it up.

What type of proof? Both technical and customer evidence:

Product Phase - Do you have a prototype? An MVP (Minimum Viable Product)? An Alpha? A Beta? Or maybe it's still just an idea sketched on a napkin. The further along you are in your product evolution, proving that you can do what you set out to do, the more likely you are to raise funding. Serial entrepreneurs with previous exits have been known to raise capital from the napkin sketch. Unless you have already sold a startup, please don't count on this happening to you.

POC - (Proof of Concept) - Validate the claims about your science or technology – offer evidence that it really works the way you say it does with data from clients and quantitative, measurable numbers.

Sales - ARR/MRR (Annual Run Rate/Monthly Run Rate or Recurring Revenue) - Clear numbers showing you warrant a high investment and higher valuation.

Logos - of customers - especially recognizable ones, grab Investors attention. It's important to note, pilots and design partners **are not** customers and should not be noted as such, unless they pay you, and they should be paying you. Ask them to pay – if they say no – ask them why (this is super important information for you to consider and make changes). Even if small, early revenue is an excellent indicator for the investors that you can get people to pay for the value you bring them.

Pipeline - Your estimated revenue for the coming year/s. Make sure you have solid numbers to base this on.

Growth - MoM/QoQ/YoY - Month over month, quarter over quarter or year over year. You must show that you are moving in the "hockey stick" vector, not just plateauing. This can and should be both about your user base and revenue growth.

MAUs/DAUs - Monthly active users or daily active users. Show steady growth in these, but PLEASE don't be tempted to pump them up with click farms or bought users, because this is easy to check on and will definitely kill your credibility.

Major Partnerships - Partnerships with complementary companies or organizations with access to a large, paying user base can amplify your product. Either as a revenue-sharing partner, a channel partner, or just because they believe in you and want to bring value to their user base. This is a very positive signal for investors, who see this as a massive pipeline with eventual revenue potential.

Note - If you landed a deal with a channel partner but haven't started distribution through them, look at a similar product they partnered with and use their sales metrics to show how you'll probably look pretty similar.

IP/Regulatory Progress - If you have a patentable technology or need regulatory approval, such as with medical or fintech startups, let them know if you have filed a patent, been granted one, or how far along you are with FDA or SEC approval. This shows significant inroads and protection.

Engagement/Stickiness - In Enterprise, the ARR has a higher bar, and sales cycles are much longer, so there are better metrics than revenue to measure your momentum. Show concrete examples from partners or paying customers on how it works for them. Gather testimonials, as discussed before.

All of these together can show that you are on your way to Product Market Fit or PMF - where you have a product customers love so much that they are willing to pay for it, again and again, to leave their old ways behind, thereby demonstrating undeniable value.

One of the Silicon Valley VC Partners I've worked with said - "When raising a Series A and trying to prove product market fit – showing big or small repeating customers that rely on your product is even more important than revenue!"

While great numbers can make a strong case for you, please steer clear of "vanity metrics" or "feel good" metrics. These metrics look impressive but don't hold any actual weight. Josh Kopelman, a partner at First Round Capital, says: "The real data is retention and repeat usage. Instrument your site to track that data."

Chris Dixon, GP at Andreessen Horowitz, agrees, stating that it's better to try to understand why you lost users and discover what excites your engaged users. He thinks it best to launch an MVP and reiterate quickly. "If you aren't embarrassed by your first product, you have launched too late," he says. Learn from mistakes, improve the product, stay lean, and keep moving forward quickly.

One more thing - be cautious with big blanket claims and definitive statements. When you use these, you automatically raise investor objections, their shields go up, and they spend their time arguing with you in their mind rather than listening to the real facts.

KYC - Know Your Customer

KYC has become a catchphrase for banks and financial institutions that must validate their customers, in order to avoid dealing with money launderers and criminals. But I suggest that we all get to know our customers very well.

Before VCs give you a few million dollars, they will most likely want to talk to a few customers of yours, that is, if you already have them. Paul Judge, Founder and CTO at Purewire Inc. and an investor, says: "It's become so sexy to pitch to investors nowadays that people forget to first go talk to customers. I have people pitch me, and when I ask what customers think about this, they tell me they don't know. So why are you talking to investors right now?" He says he needs proof that the startup is solving a "valuable problem" - meaning that customers are willing to pay for the solution.

Therefore, before you talk to VCs, it's time to speak to some key customers and get the story from them so that you can tell your "User Stories" to the VCs in an accurate way.

I'm not talking about market size, numbers and demographics here - instead, I'm talking about the intimate knowledge of your customers' stories - where they were when they 'found you' and what has changed since engaging with you.

Here are some important points to research and present:

Focus on Target Market Users - Choose clients that are part of the target audience that you are 'selling' to VCs - because these are the ones VCs seek out to talk to first.

Align with Your Clients - Find out what they like/dislike about your product. If they haven't converted to paying customers yet - why? What would need to happen to convert?

Learn the Churn - If you have clients that are no longer clients - find out why. Get candid answers and see where they migrated to and what the clients are getting that they were missing with you.

Competitive Edge - If a customer moved to you from a competitor, find out why they left the competitor and chose you. This information can strengthen your competitive edge.

Verify Testimonials - If you have testimonials on your website or deck, verify that the reviewers still stand behind their testimonials and that you have permission to use them.

It's All in the Details - Know your users' habits and how they use your product; be ready to show real-time usage analytics. Investors MUST check this box off to know your metrics are valid.

Choose What to Use - Focus on one strong usage metric that you want to emphasize - i.e. the number of return visits a day, engagement time per session, etc. Know the numbers inside and out for at least that one specific metric.

Firsthand Experience - This is a hard one, but the payoff is big: Find someone the VC knows who is a user, and tell the VC so they can ask them first-hand about their experience. In addition, if the VC's child, spouse, another entrepreneur they've invested in, etc. is an excellent potential user - offer them a free trial to get their opinion. Or if the VC is in your target market - ask them to become a user and try it out first hand.

What's the Cost to You? - Know either your Customer Acquisition Cost (CAC) and LTV Lifetime Value (LTV) or have a short-term plan to find it out if it's too early to calculate.

Let The VC Choose - Be prepared to provide a VC with contact info for clients who gave testimonials and others who didn't. Talk to them, vet them, and make sure there are no unpleasant surprises.

The more you know before, the better - you'll look more professional and avoid being stuck when they ask you questions about the customer. The more comfortable you feel answering questions and the more familiar you are with your customers - the better your pitch (not to mention your product) will be.

Market Size and Whys

One of the most prominent challenges startups struggle with on their pitch deck is what they should say about their market. Where to find the stats? What is their addressable market? This can be daunting if you're not a marketing expert doing it yourself.

You must remember — VCs are in it to win it. Talk to them with numbers. They have to be able to see the huge market potential, and you have to be able to draw an accurate picture.

The potential for your target market is an important consideration for investors. You don't necessarily have to have an all-encompassing target audience. However, there should be enough potential in terms of audience size and the lifetime value of each customer so that investors feel confident in your growth opportunities.

Investors want you to understand the available top-down market and your serviceable obtainable market. What is the current annual spend on the problem, or how much money is being lost by not having a viable solution? It's not just calculating what you can make by taking a percentage of the part and multiplying it by your cost per customer. It can be looking at the current spending on partial or siloed solutions, showing clearly that your audience is willing and able to throw money at solving the problem - and with a conservative estimate, you can show how you will take a bite of that market share. I've seen many different ways to show the market, and while there's not one right way, it's all about making it clear, and powerful.

Here are a few tips for what should be there and how to find it:

Sizing it up

Knowing your market size (potential customers) and value (total spend per year) inside and out is important. Familiarize yourself with three terms - **TAM** = Your Total Available or Addressable Market (everyone who could potentially use your product), **SAM** = Your Segmented Addressable Market or Served Available Market (Your target market within the TAM), and **SOM** = Your Share of the Market (what chunk of the SAM you will realistically reach within a few years). These numbers have to be impressive to get an investment, so if you capture a very modest share in your SOM, you still give them a significant ROI, or Return on Investment.

How do you know your TAM/SAM/SOM? Here's an example: One of my clients is in the travel deals industry. So their TAM is **all** travelers - let's say we focus on travelers in the US, that's their SAM - and their SOM is last-minute travelers - anyone booking travel under two weeks before a trip, looking for a deal. Each of the TAM/SAM/SOM should have a market size (how many users) and a value (how much is the overall spend) attached to it.

FINDING THE DATA

How on earth do you figure out all the numbers you require? If you can't afford to hire a freelance market analyst, the first obvious place is Google or other search tools, (I can see ChatGPT and the such becoming our main source of research in the coming years!) Just make sure you are citing trustworthy sources, and keeping the references so they can validate your numbers.

Try to find data from reports by noteworthy market research firms such as Gartner, Forrester, IDC, or CB Insights. Not all reports are free, yet there are free options such as gaining access through a friend studying at college.

Another fairly inexpensive way is to outsource your research - Fiverr is a fantastic marketplace where you can hire someone to research for you from $5. AskWonder.com is a great resource where you can ask analysts nearly any question and they will get back to you with a full report in about 48 hours. The more specific you are with what you're looking for, the better the results will be.

And please, like everything in your deck, make sure it's the real deal, don't be tempted to fudge the numbers. Find true numbers and their sources - don't make things up; this can seriously harm your credibility. Try to get as precise numbers as possible, but it's better not to have them at all than to make things up.

Honestly, it's not just TAM/SAM/SOM – you must be able to explain the market size and your share of it. If your market size is small, show them that it's set to grow and back this up with proof. Investors want to be excited by the overall opportunity.

From the get-go, you must set the context of the market: What's the broad theme proving why you are going to be a big company – i.e. $XXX billion moving into your space, massive fragmentation, what type of solution is missing for this market and how you fit right in, etc. If you are part of a fast-evolving market – what will maintain your uniqueness in the value chain when competition strikes?

"To Market, To Market" - The Penetration - or the Go to Market

Once you have determined your market size and your initial target market, you have to figure out how you will reach your market and acquire customers.

"Go to Market" or GTM strategy, is how you will penetrate your market. What strategies will you use and how much will it cost you to get each customer to use your product - or your CAC, using these strategies? Show that you have done your homework, that you are familiar with your market and know the best strategies to get to them at minimum cost.

To address this, you should come prepared with a detailed plan of how your business will scale over the next 12-18 months. This plan should account for your current sales cycle and customer acquisition strategies and how changes like hiring additional staff will enhance these efforts. It must also show viable Key Performance Indicators (KPIs) for the life of the runway.

Here are a few different types of strategies:

Founder/Team Network - If you and/or your team are seasoned professionals in your field, that comes with a very valuable network and Rolodex (or, for today's world, a contact list). If you can easily drop an email or pick up a phone with a high-level executive in a coveted organization that you would love to have as a client, that's fantastic and will open doors fast.

Land and Expand - If you already have pilots or clients paying you, it means you're in the door. And massive organizations are often so big that they operate like dozens of small companies, making independent decisions on which tools to use. Once you're in the door and garner their love and support in one part of the business, you can get their help expanding throughout the organization to different parts, geos, and stakeholders. You can also upsell customers with new products and features as they emerge. Once you have convinced the customer to pay you for one product that they're super happy with, the next one is a much easier sell.

Business Development - (Biz Dev) Having someone in your team who connects you with new partners or potential clients, sets up meetings, and gets you in the door utilizing their contacts. You can also do cold emailing yourself, but this is not as effective as hearing from a warm lead.

Direct Sales - Hiring a sales team to do what they were born to do - sell! This is an expensive strategy - salary expectations are high, and you will likely need to have a robust product already showing growth in order to hire great salespeople, so this is usually a post-investment strategy.

Content is King - A great strategy is content marketing, putting valuable content out to your followers which positively spreads your name, becoming known as a thought leader. This leaves them wanting more, and is a great way to gain their trust and loyalty. It's also relatively inexpensive and a way to gain significant market attention that can lead to partnerships and even acquisitions. And FYI, I have shared bits and pieces of content over the years, it has been a massive lead generation strategy, and much of the content could then be incorporated into this book!

Partner Up - Are there other businesses that need your services or have complementary services and can partner with you to do cross offerings, recommend your services to their customers and be your biggest ambassador? If the partnership is right, this doesn't have to cost you anything and can bring outstanding results. In addition, you can offer a revenue share model that sweetens the deal even more for them.

Influencer Marketing - In the era of Instagram and TikTok, we have been flooded with influencers. Everyone is suddenly an expert, garnering tens of thousands of followers, and generating massive revenue for the brands they work for - and for themselves. The secret to the influencer's success is that it's pretty close to user-generated content, or UGC. They seem like ordinary people, like you and me (unless they are Kim Kardashian), who just love using a product. If you are early on, you can look for Micro-Influencers or Nano-Influencers, with smaller audiences, who have powerful voices. They might charge less per engagement or post in return for free products. Obviously, you need to find an Influencer in the space you are working in; otherwise, their shares are not of value to you. This works exceptionally well for companies with physical products that can be shown in a user or unboxing video.

Digital Marketing –

Ads - Highly targeted sponsored posts or ads on Facebook, Instagram or TikTok can range from inexpensive to very expensive. These ads are a great way to experiment and get to know your audience. But with so many algorithm changes and Apple constantly augmenting the rules, make sure you have someone who knows what they're doing; otherwise, you can throw a lot of money out the window.

LinkedIn - A great way to share your content, and also use their paid ad system or 'inmail,' both of which are very expensive, so again, know what you're doing and have a clear strategy.

Google Adwords/SEO - They say that the best place to hide a body is on the fifth page of Google - nobody ever makes it there! The holy grail is to be found 'organically', but that still must be managed by good Search Engine Optimization (SEO) and by paying Google for their AdWords. These are expensive yet highly valuable tools, and again, I suggest working with an expert that has been recommended to you from someone with personal experience.

Email Marketing - Sending out email campaigns, newsletters, etc., can be valuable, but you must use a tool that lets subscribers opt-in or opt-out - for information privacy and security reasons. If you don't include the opt-in or opt-out option, you can find yourself marked as spam or even slapped with a lawsuit. Try to create original, exciting content that speaks to your reader. Think about the newsletters that you open and read. What makes them valuable to you? And don't overdo the frequency - that's a great way to get the reader to hit "unsubcribe."

Industry Presence - Trade shows, networking events, conferences, sponsorships - physically being there, making your presence known with a booth, including swag, or just handshakes or elbow bumps can also gather valuable leads. These can be expensive strategies, therefore make sure you're targeting highly valuable events, making the most of your spend.

Hack it - Growth hacking is a popular buzzword, and like many other buzzwords, it's essential to know what's behind the buzz so that you can provide investors with an in-depth picture of the strategy. Wikipedia defines growth hacking's goal: "To regularly conduct experiments, which can include A/B testing, that will lead to improving the customer journey, and replicate and scale the ideas that work and modify or abandon the ones that don't before investing a lot of resources."

Monica O'Hara, Growth Hacker Extraordinaire, whose company DataScore was acquired by Lyft in 2017, said:

"Finding smart avenues of growth begins with brainstorming where your target customer 'hangs out' online. Do they read certain websites? Are they active on any social channels or forums? Once you identify where they are, you can plan how to engage with them. There are tools out there that can help speed up your outreach process."

Community/Product Led Growth (PLG) - PLG is a strategy that has emerged in the past few years. It is where a company's software becomes the center of the buying journey and the customer experience. PLG lets the product and its features handle a lot of the selling. This is often driven by a community of users that are early adopters who love and evangelize the product, and foster its growth without necessarily expecting anything in return. Community managers have become an important role in startups, and I anticipate this getting even more important.

"Going Viral" - One thing to note: 'going viral' is not a strategy. By saying "oh our product/video will go viral" you are basically saying nothing. Videos go viral - some by luck and some go viral via lots of money invested into getting it seen. If you show that you have elements of virality in your product (for example, by Incentivizing shares - i.e. share with 10 friends to get a free month) then that makes more sense. But there's a delicate balance of not being too pushy when getting users to share.

Get Creative - If you can find a strategy that is unique to your product, that has a twist, and not everyone has tried, you can then sweep the market and fascinate investors. Get creative. For example - if you have two types of users - Businesses and consumers - if you can show that you will turn the businesses into your ambassadors, bringing on their existing customers - that's a neat strategy.

There are many other strategies, with new ones constantly emerging. It's important to have a strategy for every phase. Obviously, you will have fewer resources when starting, so show that you will maximize the early phases with lower cost/higher yield strategies such as social media. Then, later in the game, go for the more expensive strategies like a sales team, trade show presence, etc. Plot out your phases, your target market, and the strategy you intend to use for each phase. Know your strategies, ensure they align with the amount of money you're asking for and show Investors that you have a clear, attainable path to reach your market.

Making Friends with Competition

It always makes me smile a little when a startup says they have no competitors. On more than one occasion, I've had to awkwardly show a startup a very big competitor they'd never heard of, watch their face fall, then send them home to do some homework before proceeding. (Hey, better it happening with me than with an investor!)

First, let's get something straight - competition is a great thing! Without Jerry, we'd have no Tom; without Roadrunner, we'd have no

Coyote, and what would be the fun if Apple didn't have Google chomping at their core? But just because Apple is killing it in a particular market doesn't invalidate its competitors. There's room for all.

It's time to embrace our competition, to make friends with it. To use it to our advantage. If a market is worth having, it will have competition – you just have to explain how you will do it differently; what sets you apart? You must be 10x better or 10x cheaper to replace a current solution. What's your brilliance? What's so much better about you that leaves historical solutions in the dust? Not just the big players but the funded startups.

Another VC partner told me: "Talking about competition builds trust with VCs if you do it right. What we want to know is what you are doing differently. Why are you faster? Bigger? It's all about speed of execution – how will you compete with the big players? I'm not interested in hearing about the little startups out there; I want to know how you'll compete with the Googles and Apples of the world or the startups backed by Greylock, Sequoia or Andreessen Horowitz."

As we discussed earlier, you can briefly mention the competition right after the problem statement, so they know you will address it. At this point in the pitch, come back to it, add information from your customers, what wasn't being solved for them with other solutions, and how it is now. They want to hear you explain the competition and market to see that YOU understand it

So how do you handle competition when pitching to investors?

Know your Landscape Inside and Out - Look under every rock and tree to find your direct and indirect competitors. "Direct" means they are doing something very similar to you and targeting the same audience; "indirect" means they touch on your target audience but solve the problem differently. For example, VRBO is a direct competitor of Airbnb; however, Craigslist is an indirect competitor because they also offer short-term rentals but don't have the whole ranking and payment system in place. Even though VRBO was considered the underdog to Airbnb, that didn't stop them from being acquired way before Airbnb went public!

Competitive Intelligence - Where do you find out about your competitors? Well, Google is the obvious first stop, but there are websites like SimilarWeb that can give insights to potential competitors. The best way is to ask potential users what they currently are using (if anything) to deal with the problem you are setting out to solve.

No Talking Trash - Please, don't ever say anything bad about your competitor - you don't know who might be sitting in the room that's an investor/board member/mentor of one of your competitors. It also reflects poorly on you that you have to trash your competition to aggrandize yourself, and it leaves them thinking, "hmm, if they talk that way about a competitor, I wonder what they might say about me behind my back?" Always say something like - "What competitor A is doing is ABC, we do ABC plus we have a magic dose of XYZ..." Why are you better? What sets you apart? And please, don't underestimate or undervalue your competition – saying things like: "we've got it covered, they're no match for us..." – showing you don't take your competition seriously is an instant red flag for investors.

Build on Your Competitors' Success - If a competitor of yours was just acquired or received significant funding, use this to show how hot the market is, hint that you might be next because you have a secret sauce that they don't and make them feel that they could be missing the opportunity of a lifetime. No Investor likes to think they missed out on the next big thing. For example, I had a client building an enterprise solution with three competitors that Gartner acquired in the past 12 months. That's a pretty big signal that if he could prove his capabilities, he might be snapped up by a Gartner competitor, or even by Gartner themselves.

Show - Don't Tell - Martin Zwilling, an Angel Investor, says, "Every investor hates those large competitive analysis tables filled with check marks and red dots." Every investor I've ever spoken to agrees; DON'T do a feature check box or a Harvey Balls chart – nobody likes these, especially when you're comparing yourself to an industry giant. You want to have a visual that explains it at first glance. Here are a few good options:

The "Magic Quadrant" - A graph attributed to Gartner shows how you measure up to competition based on two main differentiators. Here's Airbnb's original competition slide:

The Magic Quadrant or 2X2

They use affordability and online transactions as the main differentiators.

I always knew that investors HATED the chart with the checks and x's showing you and your competitors. I didn't realize they felt almost as vehemently opposed to the magic quadrant (or 2X2). VCs say it bores them because everyone has it, and it always looks the same, with your company at the top right. One of the VCs even noted that a company pitching to them tried to "shake things up" and put their company on the bottom left – and everyone got mad at them.

This actually proves that, love or hate it, whether VCs admit it or not, they almost expect and even need to see the Magic Quadrant. If you are showing a 2X2 competitive matrix like this, make sure there are meaningful X/Y axes. Investors want to know in one glance that you deeply understand the landscape and the vectors are meaningful to the competition.

The "Petal Diagram" - My personal favorite. Steve Blank, serial entrepreneur, lecturer and author of Startup Owner's Manual, suggests a different approach:

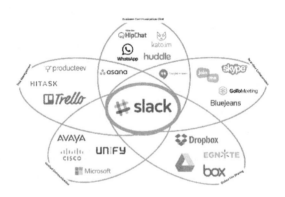

The Petal Diagram

This is where your startup is at the center of several markets that each touch on a specific aspect of your solution, and you encompass all of them. As you see in the example, the ever-popular Slack is at the center, touching on business communication/chat, collaboration, file sharing, unified communication and task management. In a way, it competes with them all, but it actually does all the things the petals do in one tool!

Note that there are only about three of the top companies in each petal - this is a good representation without overcrowding. You don't have to have five petals - even three is enough - it's a great way to solve the conundrum of having more than two metrics to measure your uniqueness.

Also, note that some of these are competitors - actual solutions that were doing something similar or partial to Slack - this shows that they can integrate with them now and kick them out of the sandbox later (which they did!). While some of these are 'Completitors' (my own made-up word), those companies will happily continue playing with Slack in the sandbox. Either way, it shows how they relate to each other.

A Marketscape - Show your competition and how you measure up on a marketscape.

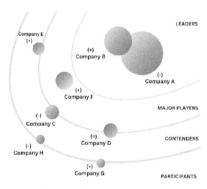

The Marketscape

Show where there are solutions and where the gaping hole is that you will fill in. As one VC Partner put it "Don't be afraid to use a little Hubris – show a dot – We're here – here's where we'll be in a few years – the biggest guys on the block" – show sector understanding and explain why you think you'll get from here to there."

Simply Show your Competitors - Have the logos of the top competitors, say a few words about them, and show that you understand what they're doing. Then talk about your uniqueness, your magic, your secret sauce – especially if you're in a very crowded space where they might be suffering from 'pitch fatigue'.

Talking about the competition can be an emotionally charged part of the pitch. It feels like a personal attack on your 'baby'. It's not. Investors are looking for a good response. The most important thing - keep your cool, breathe, count to 10 before answering a difficult question. Remember - Investors are watching to see how you deal with challenging questions even more than they are listening for your answer.

MONETIZATION - IT'S ALL ABOUT THE MONEY

I am a self-proclaimed words woman. I am not a numbers woman. As my dear husband put it, I'm proof that you can be very successful without algebra :) (I cannot argue with that). However, I want to outline the monetization models and what they mean in layperson terms that even non-numerical people like me will get. There are many excellent references and professionals out there that can explain it in depth. Here's my basic attempt:

Business model, revenue model, revenue streams - there are many terms to describe this lifeblood of your startup. Let's make some order out of the chaos, thanks to Founders Institute:

A revenue stream - is a company's single source of revenue. Depending on the size, a company can have zero or many revenue streams.

A revenue model - is the strategy of managing a company's revenue streams and the resources required for each revenue stream.

A business model - is the structure comprising all aspects of a company, including revenue model and revenue streams, and describes how they all work together.

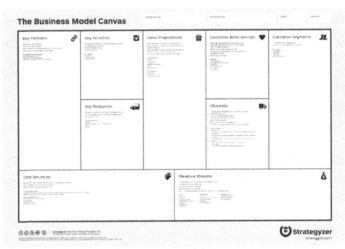

The Business Model Canvas

The Business Model Canvas is one of many ways to plot out your business/revenue models. - The template was designed by Alexander Osterwalder in 2005 and is an excellent tool for plotting and tracking.

There are many different types of revenue models to choose from - here are a few examples:

Subscription (SaaS) Model - The Software as a Service (SaaS) model is loved by both companies and investors. This is a monthly or annual subscription that often renews automatically and gives a clear picture of recurring revenue. VCs will say that you aren't VC investable if you don't have recurring revenue. This does not mean you aren't a great company, but VCs want to see products that have a repeatability of income, which keeps the money flowing in – not a one-time purchase.

Freemium Model - A "free" model where new customers are welcome to try the basic version of the product for free. This is a great way to grow a user base who will hopefully fall in love with your product and convert to paying users, either when the trial period is up or wanting to use more advanced features. This can be a real misnomer - because the actual revenue is from the "-ium" part, or the add-on services, premium features, access to data, etc.

Marketplace Model - You connect two (or more) sides in a transaction, and you get a transaction fee for any deal completed on your platform.

Affiliate or Ads Model - You have a free product, but you make revenue from ads on the feed or using affiliate links as you drive your users to these other sites. Usually, users can opt to move to a paid version to remove ads.

Data Play - This is what many companies drive towards - as they grow their presence and user base, they gather invaluable insights about user behavior. They can analyze this data and extract highly valuable insights for brands and companies, to help those brands to understand their end user better. The data is usually anonymized, and this will likely be a subscription model. It's a tremendous ancillary source of revenue, one that takes a long time to achieve.

All investors know that business models are fluid and can completely change as you move between phases, so don't sweat it too much - but you must have educated reasoning behind your business models so Investors see you have given it serious thought.

When it comes to numbers, revenue projections, deal sizes, and other calculations, it's imperative to know your numbers inside out. Even if you don't come from a business or finance background, you must think like a businessperson. When you're at the stage of speaking to a VC, you need to show that you have business acumen and that you are able to demonstrate that you will have a detailed command of your numbers. You will be handling (a lot of) their money, and they want to know it's in good hands.

Know the milestones you will deliver with the funds you raise – Look ahead 18 months – where will you be with pilots? Monthly Recurring Revenue (MRR) or Annual Recurring Revenue or Annual Run Rate (ARR) , forecast, customers, employees, users, expenses. Then work backwards. Map it and build the onramp that takes you there – even if you have to massage your KPIs (Key Performance Indicators like revenue, growth, users, etc.) or burn rate (what you're spending each month on salaries, servers, marketing, etc.), at least, you'll know, even if it's only based on assumptions. Even if these numbers change - it will be apparent to you what you are expected to achieve by the time you're raising your next round.

A VC Partner said to me that startups should: "Think about the operating model that you will/should have – you are a financial product. What that means is that the market only cares about the slope of growth and Earnings Before Interest (EBITDA), Taxes, Depreciation, and Amortization, an indicator of profitability) or can you create profit? Have a clear financial model that you can track. What will your Profits and Losses (P&L) look like – even though you're years away from it, show us that you went through the mental exercise and you truly understand where you're heading."

Opportunization - Make them feel the FOMO.

This is likely the most important part of this book. It can give you the edge your deck needs, so read carefully.

Numbers are just dandy. But as Reid Hoffman says: "Frequently, young entrepreneurs put in slides that show their business' total addressable market (TAM) to establish some credibility. Most investors don't trust the sources of that information, so entrepreneurs aren't establishing huge credibility by saying they've claimed a market with a huge TAM."

So what can you do to persuade them, in spite of or in addition to the market size?

Investors often suffer from Fear of Missing Out (FOMO), and nobody wants to feel that they missed out on the next big thing, so you need to push their triggers. Investors receive at least 100 pitch decks a week; they might read them all and might not. They may like your idea, but you need Investors to care right now and see the immediate relevance if you want them to invest.

So what should you be talking about? Trends and opportunities! Why are you a hot investment opportunity now, and what backs that up? Think of the Eisenhower Matrix, where tasks are split by importance and urgency. Your story might convince them of its importance, but they'll pick something else if it shows it's urgent too.

There are a few ways you can do this:
1. Can you prove there is high demand for what you're doing?
2. Are people willing to spend money to solve this pain? Can you prove this with numbers?
3. Are there underserved trends?
4. Has the law/regulation shifted to allow space/demand for new entrants?
5. Is there a wider economic shift you can capitalize on?

Are there signals in the market showing that others see it as hot? (i.e. major rounds or acquisitions of others in your competitive landscape)

Hopin is one of the fastest-growing European startups ever. It went from being worth $200 million in late 2019 to over $6 billion in 2021. Investors fought each other for the honor of investing because Hopin was perfect for what happened to the world in 2020. Their virtual conference event software could replicate real-life interactions while everyone was stuck at home in lockdown.

If Hopin's Founder had shown his pitch deck to investors five years before, there would have been far less of a frenzy. But they were in the right time at the right place and were able to change their story to make it a very timely investment opportunity.

Fun story - Brian Chesky, Co-Founder and CEO of Airbnb, released a blog with seven rejection emails from investors when they were raising at a super low valuation. And these astonishing emails said things to the tune of:

"Sounds interesting, not something we really do here…"
"The potential market opportunity doesn't seem large enough…"
"It's not in one of our prime target markets…"
"We've not been able to get excited about travel as a category"

(Brian ends this beautifully by saying, "Next time you have an idea and it gets rejected, I want you to think of these emails." This is SO important for all you founders out there on this rollercoaster ride to hear!)

When Airbnb finally IPO'd, the company's valuation was $47 billion. Imagine what the writers of those rejection emails felt? If only they could have known…

Bessemer Ventures, meanwhile, takes its losses with a bit of humor, displaying an "Anti-Portfolio" that honors the companies they missed investing in. (Yes, you guessed it, Airbnb is there too alongside Google and some other biggies.) But what if they could see into the future and have a company excite them enough to show that brand of potential? That's where trends and opportunities come in.

It's you who needs to help them! Hand them the crystal ball, turn the FOMO fire up, and make them believe the time for you is now.

You can't just sell the market: you have to sell your business, too, but the aim of selling the market to investors is to highlight the opportunity they have on their hands. The truth is that a good idea isn't enough; it's only part of the equation. It's necessary to convince an investor that you have the right idea, that you're the right person and this is the right time.

That last factor is vital: VCs won't invest in something with little urgent need in the world and wouldn't have gotten to where they are if they made a habit of doing so. Over nearly two decades of looking at pitch decks, I'm convinced that this is a major secret to your success, your 'silver bullet'.

FIND YOUR SILVER BULLET - AND SHOOT IT FAST!

If you want to convince investors that they should invest in you, you need to find your 'silver bullet' as soon as possible. Each time you go into a pitch without it, you're not making the most of an opportunity. Once you have created a sense of urgency for your startup's product, don't be surprised if you find yourself picking up the phone finding an enthusiastic investor on the other end.

Most founders fail to make investors believe there is a consumer base out there that's longing for their product at that moment; when I've seen startup founders nail that 'urgency effect', however, the room's atmosphere completely shifts. If you can find the silver bullet that cuts through all the noise, your pitch will level up.

I always try to put three major trends in this section, and the convergence of these is what produces the urgency effect. They might differ slightly from industry to industry, but you'll get the idea:

BEHAVIORAL TRENDS

Attitudes and tastes worldwide are constantly shifting, which is a nightmare for established companies, but a gift for startups. Whenever behavior changes happen en masse, some doors shut, but others open. This is a time when you can truly seize the opportunity. If I take a wide scan of behavioral changes happening in the world over the past few years, there are a few standouts:

Covid-19 - has been a massive driver, especially in pushing people to adopt e-commerce faster than expected, new models of working, living, digital health, and so much more. These shifts will continue to have ripples well into the next decade.

Supply chain issues - are driving the need to maximize material sourcing and find more local manufacturing options here in the U.S.

Climate change and sustainability - are top-of-mind issues, especially among millennials and Gen-Z, the shift of consumer patterns away from the excesses of older generations and toward environmentally-responsible products, including meat alternatives, ethical sourcing for fashion, eCommerce, and anything that contributes to reducing carbon emissions.

If you can back up the perceived change in behavior with hard numbers in a pitch, expect investors to sit up and pay close attention to whatever you say for the rest of the presentation. For example, armed with the fact that a third of millennials are willing to pay more for sustainable products (according to the Global Sustainability Study 2021 by Simon-Kucher & Partners), investors will want to see how they can benefit from this trend.

This is merely a partial list to drive home a point: find the behavioral change, shift or pattern in your industry and see if and how your product or service responds to it. If a new trend pops up

(COVID certainly caught us by surprise), see if you can pivot your product to better serve the burning need du jour.

REGULATORY

Behavioral change usually doesn't happen overnight (well, in pandemic times it seemed to), but regulatory moves can force change whether we like it or not. There have been many instances when governments have changed the rules by which the private sector plays, producing winners and losers. You just have to convince potential investors that you'll be one of the winners.

The web is a particular magnet for regulators as they try to play catch up with the rapid rate of innovation. Here are a few examples:

Accessibility requirements - and the potential for litigation led to the rise of companies that aimed to solve various problems for companies, including proving compliance with such requirements (or risking consequential fines). To investors, it might only have been obvious that the world needed such companies once the regulation said so.

Information privacy - General Data Protection Regulation (GDPR) and The California Consumer Privacy Act (CCPA) are major laws enacted over the last few years. These have spawned many startups aimed at helping organizations make sure they stay within their stipulations. Demand for such services was both immediate and overwhelming, meaning the growth potential was incredible.

Sustainability - Not just a behavioral trend - this is getting real! In 2022, a series of regulations rolled out: ISSB Sustainability Disclosure, EU Taxonomy's Climate Delegated Act, EU's Sustainable Finance Disclosure Regulation (SFDR), and Europe's new Corporate Sustainability Reporting Directive (CSRD). These are aimed at holding companies accountable for sustainability practices and reporting. Companies will have to maintain compliance and if you have a technology that helps them, you will be in high demand.

As an example of regulatory trend success, I worked with a client who had developed a GDPR solution for financial institutions a good three years before it was set to go into effect. Investors just didn't get the 'Why'. But when GDPR rolled out, suddenly companies like Facebook were getting hit with billions of dollars in fines and also being blocked in the EU. You can bet that they needed rapid solutions that would scale fast and get them GDPR compliant. And guess what? My client was acquired for a very nice sum. And since investors (save a few Angels) hadn't had the foresight to see this coming, my client was almost entirely non-diluted and he and his partners took home nearly the entire payload. Good for them!

You need to act fast if you believe a regulatory change is your silver bullet. If you've spotted an opportunity, it's a safe bet that others have too, so have a pitch deck prepared so you can meet investors before the issue is already front-page news.

HEAT IN THE SPACE

This last pathway to urgency is the cheekiest but potentially the most effective. To make use of it, you've got to be obsessed with your market and know everything that's happening with the companies sharing your space. If you can show an investor that the sector is heating up, then you can touch on their FOMO receptors. Investors tend to invest by signals from the market - and if they see their peers throwing money at a particular industry, it's an excellent indicator that they should follow suit.

It doesn't matter if a competitor is doing well when the market is in its infancy. As history has taught us, the first mover is often someone other than the one who sees long-term success (Just ask Myspace or Bebo. Who? Exactly my point). Heat presents a strong signal to an investor that your company fixes a problem that needs fixing, and that through you they can gain exposure to market growth as a whole. This signal creates urgency because if they keep talking to different companies for too long, the fear is that they might be too late in capitalizing on the early stages of growth. When Investors know their competitors are making big bets, they want to avoid being the odd one out and losing money through indecisiveness.

Look at your competitors - has anyone just raised massive funding? Has anyone been acquired or gone public? If so, that's great! It can signal to Investors that you are the next hot thing. These factors show that money is pouring into the industry and that other investors are confident in future prospects (and the result can often be bidding wars).

Is there a quote from a major source like Gartner or Forrester saying that this is the year for a startup like yours? Grab that quote! I recently worked with a company raising their Series B, and they had a quote from one of the big names mentioning them, side by side with big players like IBM - it was a nice stamp of approval for investors to see.

After saying for years that this is the silver bullet for your pitch – finally, I had a VC partner back me up on it and say: "Tell them Why now! Why is your product/solution/technology something whose time has come? What's the enabling factor? What are the trends pointing towards it? And if you didn't exist – what trend would still be happening? What is the bigger trend that you are hooked into?"

Don't think for one minute that Investors must already know it - they might and they might not - you are there to ensure the dots are connected and the heat is on.

TEAM WORKS - BUILD ON YOUR CREDIBILITY.

Now we arrive at the 'credibility' piece - your team. These are the people that are set to execute this beautiful vision of yours. You need to show investors exactly why they are the team to do it. They can truly be your "unfair advantage" - their experience, knowledge, and skills are a huge part of your success and a strong card in your deck.

The question of where to put the team slide comes up often. To me, it's the same reasoning as the brag slide: If you have a strong team with multiple exits, extensive industry experience and logos of credible places that you have been affiliated with, you can lean into your team's credibility by making your second slide about them. Boast about how capable they are and make your audience see that this is a powerhouse team who can execute the vision you are selling.

Suppose you have pulled C-Level members away from big companies. In that case, this is a highly credible signal to investors that they truly saw something in you and were willing to walk away from the comfort of their cushy corporate job and get into the trenches with you.

If your team is young, inexperienced, and first-time entrepreneurs, as hungry and scrappy as they might be, you'll be better off putting them towards the end of Act III. (The business section, the one you're currently in ;))

Stage Venture Partners, an LA Based Early Stage Fund, says they have three primary questions regarding the team: Can they ship, sell, and hire? A great team slide should be able to answer these questions in just one glance.

It's important to remember that your team slide is not a resume - you don't have to list all job experience or education. It's too detailed and overwhelming and the investors aren't hiring them, they're looking to see why they are the team to bring your vision to success. I leave the qualifications off because it's usually highly imbalanced across the various members.

On the other hand, not having anything about each member can be just as harmful.

Who should you have on the slide? There is no need to have the entire team if you already have employees. Put the founding team, C-Level, and a few prominent advisors as you acquire them. As you mature, you will likely need a separate slide for the advisory board. You can write "supported by a team of six Full-Time Employees (FTEs)" just to show that you have additional team members - score - you have hired great talent!

What you should have on the slide:

A picture - of each team member - a high-quality image against a neutral background that doesn't look like it was cut from a wedding picture or vacation album. Our phones have very high-quality cameras nowadays, so do a mini-photoshoot if needed.

Title - of each member.

Assets - three to four bullets that highlight the team member's greatest assets, accomplishments and what they bring to the table.

Exits - if anyone has led or held a key position in a company that exited - I would proudly display the "Exit Badge" on their picture - if they did it once, they could do it again!

Logos - of places the team member worked for, or, were affiliated with.

Stage Venture Partners created a simple yet effective example of a team slide that is both striking and informative at the same time:

Stage Venture Partners example team slide

Act IV - Moving Forward (aka The Hero's Next Moves)

We are on the home stretch now! Woot! You got through the extremely laborious part of putting together your business stats and numbers. Now it's time to drive towards what we know you're here for - the Ask. But before you get there, you can do a few things to sweeten the pie and make it easy for Investors to say yes.

Once our hero has proven they have a viable strategy to conquer the villain, we need to know what comes next. What does the future look like? Will there be other, bigger villains to conquer? How big can it scale?

The Roadmap - How far you'll go

Moneytime is getting close. Now you just need to wrap up a few loose ends, one of them being what will the life of the runway (the time this funding will give you to grow your company - you know, like the length of a runway that a plane has to land and not crash and burn?) looks like. Here, you want to give major product and sales/revenue milestones. You should not go into every detail of what you do; chunk up to the major moments so that Investors can see what's achievable in this period.

All early-stage VCs are constantly imagining your next round – as you're talking, they're thinking through the next 18 months and when you will be ready to raise again.

A VC Partner told me: "Once I write a check – I'm on the hook to help you raise your next Round. Having clarity on what you'll achieve in the next 18 months is super important for me to see how you'll raise your next round and how I'll bring on board the best investors for you."

Investors have a responsibility for your next round too! They either need to invest or have a good reason why they can't, like phase, check size etc. Investors need to be able to extend you to their investor network so they can bring in the big guns to co-invest with you.

What Should be There?

The roadmap can be a timeline with the MAJOR milestones of the next 18-24 months. You can have 2 lines - one on product milestones, the other on KPIs in Sales, marketing, etc.

On these timelines:

Talk about what your MRR will be: Give them the roadmap to enable them to see whether you can execute it. What are the KPIs you've already hit and KPIs you'll deliver? It's not fun and games; it's a real business. You don't have to go into every single detail of what you will do - stick to actual achievements.

Talk about your raise and your metrics: What's your 'proxy for revenue' – meaning, what are the numbers for your current DAU, WAU and MAU (Daily, Weekly and Monthly Active Users) and how that will continue to grow and bring in revenues after you raise. If you have absolute numbers of growth, users, and revenues.

One of the mottos I've adopted is "Under promise, over deliver." Be realistic about what you can achieve, and then you can pleasantly surprise them when you exceed expectations. At the same time, make sure that you are justifying the funding you are asking for with significant movement.

The Big Vision - The 'Why' reprised.

Remember 'the Why' statement that we started with? As I promised, here's another great spot to put it in. When you state it at the beginning, it should elicit an emotional, gut response in your listeners. Something that intrigues them and grabs their attention. Now it's time to tie it all together with a nice bow.

This section is where you set up the potential for a sequel, or your next round. With a roadmap, you can impress investors with how you plan to use their hard-earned funding and explain where you're going next. But, maybe this pitch for this specific product or phase is only one step on a much bigger journey — and now you want to go full circle back to where you started — the North Star and how you plan to get there. This should get Investors even more excited about the future than they are about the present.

By this point, Investors have pretty much seen the entire play, and as we get ready for the final curtain call, there's one more 'Hero's song' to sing. Usually, if you're at a Broadway musical, it's a dramatic reprise of a song sung earlier, and then the whole cast joins in, holds hands and ends with a beautiful crescendo that brings the audience to their feet.

Likely, there won't be a standing ovation for you, but you can employ this same dramatic ending. Now that we've shown the 'Why', the 'What' and the 'How', plus how you'll make money in the process, it's time to send them on a little journey into the future.

Bring back the vision statement, but now you can make it clearer. You can say - "but this is all the first step in the process - where we are heading is_____ " (insert why/vision). Then you can speak about upcoming features, products, geos etc. that you plan to launch. Tell them how that will take you to the grand vision, where every startup aims to be - a groundbreaking, earth-quaking, mind-shaking company that has truly moved the needle.

Again, I know this is not where you're at yet, and aren't claiming to be. But by painting this big, visionary picture, you're helping them to imagine just how big it can be, and backed by all the stats, numbers and quotes you've provided throughout the pitch, they might just see it with you and want to join the journey. And then it's a great segue into asking for the funding to help you reach the next milestone on the way to greatness.

THE ASK - IT ALL COMES DOWN TO THIS

This part of the story is all about showing what could happen with a successful investment and launch. Once your hero has defeated the villain, what happens next?

It's the moment we've all been waiting for - the big ask, the funding requirements, the reason you've gone through all four acts of the play. Often, when I get the rough draft of a pitch deck from a client, it either doesn't have an Ask slide (Seriously? What do you think you're doing there?) Or, there's a range like - "Seeking $3-$5 million. Um, is this a multiple-choice question? An auction? No! There's a huge difference between three million and five million dollars, and you will hurt yourself if you're unclear about how much you need and what you need it for.

You should leave no room for ambiguity about what your Ask is. Use a clear statement starting with, "Seeking $XX million for:" Then, include the primary allocations such as Product development, sales and marketing, team expansion, etc. You don't have to list things like salaries, legal and admin - you also don't need a full Profits and loss report (P&L) - they will want more details later, but these should be the big ticket items you will be spending on.

Stick to things like, what's the product pipeline and the marketing strategy? How far along will you be when you need to raise your next round? You don't have to detail the entire monthly burn rate, but give them an idea of how you will use the money so they know you're raising enough to keep you covered until you're ready to raise your next round.

Then, and this is important, something that most founders neglect to put on, state your 'Round Objective' — what you believe the money will help you achieve in what timeframe. Tell them the major milestones you'll hit in the next few years, how you plan to get there, and the KPIs that will reflect this success. Basically, the summary of the highlights on the roadmap. Critically put the round objective and major milestones together and explain how the money Investors give you will help you to achieve your targets. Be as precise as possible, because many startups mismanage their funds.

What shouldn't be on an Ask slide? I would never put a straight-up valuation on the slide. What if they have a higher or lower valuation in mind? This could show misalignment. There's a time for valuations - and it's with lawyers over a term sheet. Why start unnecessary arguments now?

Another thing that shouldn't be on the slides is an exit strategy. Never volunteer that information. Gordon Daugherty, a startup advisor and investor, says investors are looking for a large ROI. And if your Exit strategy is planned for too soon or too late, you are signaling that investors will see a small, fast ROI or a potentially big but very distant ROI. Both scenarios can harm your chances at an investment.

If they ask you what your exit strategy is, your answer should be to the effect of "We are fully focused on building a strong, lasting company. That's our core mission and passion." Investors really want to hear that you're not looking for a quick sell and you're in it for the long haul with the big payoff.

While you don't necessarily want to spell it out on a slide, you must have a well-thought-out Exit Strategy, so that if they keep asking you have a few "well if you insist..." answers. Another VC partner told me: "I need to be able to envision Act I, Act II, Act III – where are you going? Even if you fail, will you have a nice exit by then?" (I love it when they use storytelling lingo!)

38% of startups fail because they run out of money. You don't want investors to think you'll be one of them.

How much should you raise? As I already told you, I'm a words woman, not a numbers person, but you should always raise enough that you have funding for 12-18 months. The last thing Investors want is to see you on the road again in 6 months, raising ANOTHER round.

KEY INVESTMENT MERITS - OR WHY YOUR AUDIENCE WILL LOVE YOUR HERO

You've told Investors the story, and probably half an hour or more has passed, and while we hope you've enamored them at this point, we want to remind Investors exactly what makes you a great investment opportunity. Don't neglect the final slide, which is a golden opportunity to summarize your story! The "Key Investment Merits" or "Why Us Why Now?" slide should give Investors key takeaways.

When Investors get up from the table, what are the key highlights you want them to remember? Drop the five to six most persuasive investor benefits to drive home that this is an excellent chance for them to invest in a solution with incredible potential. Things like: huge market, strong team, converging trends, massive growth, and large pipeline - these are the moments you want to solidify into Investors brains as they continue to mull over the opportunity. This is not something new, rather the "best of" your deck, and when repeated, like your story, should stick.

Hopefully, at this point, you're hearing something to the effect of "let's set an additional meeting…"

A Note About Slides

How many times have you sat down to a presentation and seen a slide overloaded with dozens of bullets and size eight fonts, and your brain just went, "Nooo! Make it stop!!" Brad Boyer, my longtime mentor, used to call this "Death by Sui-slide."

When you overload your slides with text, you signal to people that your written words are more important than what you're saying because we've been conditioned to read what's on a blackboard or whiteboard from school days. And when someone is speaking, and you're reading - guess what? You're not capable of listening to them.

The visual cues of the words are tapping into the listening or auditory area of your brain. If you're one of those readers that also recite the words to themselves (like I am), you are simply incapable of even hearing what the speaker is saying. Researchers call this "inattentional deafness." You may be the world's greatest multitasker, but if you are both trying to read and listen - something will be sacrificed.

Guy Kawasaki talks about a 10-slide model, saying "If you must use more than ten slides to explain your business, you probably don't have a business." Sorry Guy, I'm not a fan of this statement. Because in my experience, what happens when people read this is that they try to cram EVERYTHING they have to say onto ten slides. When they do this, the slides start to look like eye charts you'd read at the DMV when you renew your license, and I don't think that's what Guy meant for us to do. Paring the words down is a tough thing to learn; it's an art form.

When people ask me how many slides should be in an investor presentation, I tell them that there is no correct number. My rule of thumb is "One Big Idea Per Slide." I'd rather see you have more slides with less on them than fewer slides that make your audience's eyes water. And you should have just enough content written on the slides to give them the essence of the message and keep you on track without overloading it. Even better, you can write your one big idea as a headline or the title/footer of your slide.

Nancy Duarte, who I consider the mother of all storytelling, says "An audience can't listen to your presentation and read detailed, text-heavy slides at the same time (not without missing key parts of your message, anyway). So make sure your slides pass what I call 'the glance test': People should be able to comprehend each slide in about three seconds."

Duarte compares it to looking at a billboard as you're driving - you can't stop on a highway to read details - it's a glance, got it, visceral reaction, keep going.

As you take all of the advice you have learned so far and dive into the actual writing of your deck, I don't want you to be concerned that you have too many slides; I want you to make clean, crisp slides that they "get" right away. Think of Steve Jobs and Tim Cook's presentations - one number, one concept - the rest they talk about, and they are (were) riveting.

But what, you ask, about the people that want the deck sent out to read later? Will they get the point if you're not there to explain it? If the slides are powerful enough and have great visuals, with one key concept, then likely they should be able to. If not, you can create a send-out, or teaser deck with a bit more text to support the visuals. But please, don't punish your live audience by making them read mounds of data for the off chance that someone will read your deck later.

The Way it Looks is Half the Story

For years, I've been trying to persuade startups that it's worth investing in the graphic design of a presentation. If your pitch deck slides look shoddy, this is a reflection of your product, your brand, and your company. Often I get scoffed at and told that investors don't care how it looks as long as the company is great. Having been a fly on the wall at many pitch sessions with Silicon Valley Venture

Partners and hearing them tear into startups with awful-looking slides has validated this for me. All companies with slides that weren't up to par were chastised. They said that the slides must match the aesthetic of the product.

How the slides look matters more than you think. Think about it - when you're brought a dish at a restaurant, you first "feast with your eyes," probably snap a few Instagram-worthy pics and then dig in. If it were all just slopped on a plate, though it might taste great, you would have a hard time stomaching it - and it definitely won't be IG-worthy.

So, hire a graphic designer. I have a few great ones I've been working with for years, which I am happy to share their details with you. Alternatively, you can get your UI person to work some magic on your slides as well. If you are very early stage or very lean on budget, there are excellent tools out there: Pitch.com, Slidebean, Beautiful.ai and also, Canva. You don't have to spend a fortune or be a gifted designer to have a great-looking deck, but you have no excuse for a deck that looks crappy. You can't say you're building a $1 billion product and bringing us $1-looking slides.

UPPING YOUR PITCH GAME - THE POLISH THAT MAKES THE DIFFERENCE

Phew! You did it! You built a phenomenal deck. You're pumped! You feel your story comes through, and you are showing yourself in the best light possible! What now?

Now the 'fun' in fundraising begins. And it's anything but fun. It's draining, tumultuous, confusing, exciting and exhausting all together. If you prepare for a six-month (maybe longer) journey, and keep breathing, nothing will stop you.

You will hear many no's, hopefully, a few resounding yesses. You will also get ENDLESS advice regarding your deck. Different investors and advisors will tell you that a certain slide should be in and another one shouldn't. Trust me, if you create a new slide for each note you get from every random person, you will end up with a bloated 'patchwork pitch' that will become a mess. Listen to Investors advice, thank them for it and then ask yourself what you really think about it. You can create a slide for it in backup or add a line or two about it. But likely, unless you have heard the feedback from numerous people, you shouldn't be putting another slide into your deck.

Where do we go from here? Here are a few more tips before we say goodbye.

Now that you have the Perfect Pitch Deck - How to get VC meetings

When it comes to innovation, Mark Zuckerberg's "move fast and break things" is a great mantra, but the investment world isn't quite the same. You might only get one chance to meet an investor who could transform your business, and you don't want to blow it. Prepare in advance, and you'll reduce the possibility of mistakes and increase your chances of getting that all-important funding.

Securing a meeting with an investor is notoriously tricky, but there is such a thing as being too fast to get connected. If you aren't adequately prepared, you can burn your one shot to make a great first impression.

If you aren't lucky enough to have the right connections, getting a meeting with an investor may feel impossible. The founders I've worked with are split on what they have found to be the most difficult piece in their financing journey: landing a meeting with an investor or convincing an investor to invest at said meeting. Some entrepreneurs struggle for months trying to get a single investor to answer their messages.

Failure to secure a meeting with a VC is not always a reflection of your startup's potential. Investors receive multiple pitch decks and emails every day. It could just be that you're using the wrong contacting strategies. This is fixable.

A VC once told me they see so many great companies that they look for the little flaws as a signal to say no. Taking extra time to ensure you get the small details right before the meeting can make all the difference.

Here are some tips for getting that all-important meeting to find funding for your startup and making sure you're ready for the meetings you secure:

TWEAK YOUR LINKEDIN PROFILE

It shouldn't be surprising that a potential Investor's first stop will be your LinkedIn profile. Look at mutual connections who could vouch for you, your work history and your ever-important summary.

You can do more than a generic sentence or a few bullets about yourself. Give some thought to the summary, and tell the story, not of what you've done, but rather WHO YOU ARE - What is at the core of your values, assets, and skills? What's the theme that connects your work history? Where does your passion come through? Throw in a favorite quote for some interesting flavor. Remember, Investors are looking to invest in great technologies - and great people!

Make sure there are no gaps in positions you've held; this is a great time to reach out to former colleagues or managers to ask them for a recommendation - not just an endorsement, but a genuine recommendation of your work. You'd be surprised how many people will agree to write a recommendation, though, as with testimonials from customers, often they need a few friendly reminders. These recommendations are worth their weight in gold!

Do your homework

There is always a never-ending line of startup founders knocking on an investor's door. Many of these entrepreneurs are competent and have good business plans, but investors are human and have limits on how many meetings they can schedule per day. They must be highly selective with whom they spend their time because their time is so valuable.

Before approaching any investor, you should make a "hit list." a spreadsheet of whom you want to talk to. Collect all relevant information here. You want to answer the following questions to ensure they are the right people to contact:

What vertical do they invest in? The more aligned they are with the focus of your startup, the more likely they will ask you for a meeting. For example, don't approach an Enterprise SaaS investor if you've created a dating app.

What stage do they invest in? Some investors prefer to work with mature, growth stage companies, so if your company is just starting out, there's no point in contacting them now.

What geographical region do they invest in? Don't waste your time crafting a pitch to someone who never invests outside of Silicon Valley if you're based in London. Yes, the pandemic has shuffled the cards on this, so you can try, but focus first on investors in your geographic region or those looking to invest in your area.

Who is in their portfolio? If they have invested in companies that are similar to yours, then you'll need to investigate further. Is there a way for companies to benefit from each other? You want to be sure that you aren't competing directly with anyone in their existing portfolio. It puts them (and you) in a conflict of interest situation, and if they can't see any synergies, they will pass on you.

In addition, be sure to check out Investors website and any interviews or podcasts they have available online. It can give you an insight into their style and personality, so you are able to approach them in the right manner.

The worst thing you can do is burn a bridge by making a silly mistake. Misspelling someone's name in a letter or getting the name of the firm they represent wrong shows a lack of attention to detail—and that's not a desirable trait to have when you're asking for your money. It could mean your email is instantly moved to their junk folder. You should research every investor you'd like to reach out to, then customize your messages.

Focus on personal introductions

A common mistake of first-time founders is trying to go directly to meet an investor without first engaging in the wider community. If Investors have already heard good things about you from someone in their network before they've talked to you, then you have a considerable head start. You get points for how you land on their desk. Investors are human, and, like everyone else, the opinions of the people they trust can influence Investors' decision-making.

Investors do not exist in a bubble. They have their trusted advisors, founders whom they've already invested in, and other investors who are their friends. Reaching out to these third parties may be easier than directly contacting the investors themselves. If you can be introduced and recommended to an investor by someone they know and trust, you'll have a head start over others getting a meeting. If those connections like you and believe in your project, they may put you in touch with whoever has invested in their companies.

The founder who introduces you will have been through the same process and will have a strong understanding of the investor's personality.

Alternatively, if you're not the right fit for an investor, but they like you and your product, they can champion you to other investors and get you in the door.

Creating organic relationships where people do not feel they are being used is crucial. You should bond with people over your shared passions and try to add value wherever possible.

Hopefully, you'll find people with the "pay it forward" spirit and then get into the karma game when you're on the other side.

THE EMAIL BLURB

When reaching out to investors, you need to have a brief, yet powerful, email. You can use my own elevator pitch format of the problem/solution and an exciting tidbit about an accomplishment or the market (more on that later).

Don't just send a generic, technobabble paragraph that needs to be read five times to understand. (trust me, they won't) Make it interesting; make them curious enough to want to meet you. And if someone graciously agrees to make introductions, don't make them work hard. Have an intro email ready - written in the third person so they can simply copy and paste. Here's a good format:

Hi _____
It's my pleasure to introduce _____ (founder name), CEO of
_____ (company name)
INSERT A FEW SENTENCES ABOUT THE PROBLEM
INSERT A FEW SENTENCES ABOUT THE SOLUTION
INSERT A FEW SENTENCES ABOUT THE TRACTION/MOMENTUM
I'll let you take it from here.
Best,
Kind Introducer

Not only will they appreciate the fact that you've done the heavy lifting for them, it will help them move faster, and also, it gives you control over the narrative - because likely they will not edit it, rather send it as is.

MAKE A TEASER DECK

VCs are busy people, so you don't want to attach a 20-slide investor pitch deck in your first email to them. Instead, create a teaser deck with only five to eight slides, and pay particular attention to the first slide to ensure they read the rest. With a teaser deck, an investor should have enough information to decide whether or not you're worth inviting to a meeting.

Things change so fast that your deck might be out of date quickly (hopefully, due to excellent traction). Sending a teaser deck with your pitch email gives a potential investor a better idea of what your company does without needing to contact you.

Sending a teaser deck also works because you're making their life easier. Rather than needing to look you up or arrange a meeting, Investors have the information they want available to them straight away. The brevity is crucial, so you don't demand too much of their time. The email should include an excellent intro blurb that will excite any investor who opens it. (See above section on Email Blurb)

As well as making the investor's decision easier, the teaser deck also saves you from meeting with an investor who isn't the right fit. This stops you from chasing dead ends, and you know if someone has read it, they are a better opportunity, because they already know enough to make an informed decision about wanting to meet you and hear more.

Don't Pass the Expiration Date

From the moment you make public that you are seeking

investment, you turn over an hourglass of about six months. Hopefully, you can get the funding you want in that timeframe. If an investor sees you have been trying and failing to raise money for more than six months, they may worry that something is wrong with your startup since you have not attracted other investors. So don't set yourself up for technical failure - when you start your round is crucial. For example, starting a raise in mid-November with the holidays coming up is not a great time.

A fix for this issue is to not officially 'launch' your round and instead reach out first to investors on your "B-list" to get some friendly meetings and advice from people you realize are not likely to invest in you. These meetings may surprise you with the new connections you make and the solid practice you get pitching. Save your top wish list of investors for when you're ready to really put yourself out there.

FOLLOWING UP

It's essential to follow up after a meeting, not just because it's the polite thing to do, but because Investors are busy people and believe it or not, you aren't the only thing on their minds. You have to be persistent! Elizabeth Yin, Partner at Hustle Fund, writes that as an entrepreneur, she was afraid of bugging Investors too much, but as an Investor, she is so busy that she often doesn't notice when someone has pinged her three times. She suggests following up when you say you will, then if you haven't heard back, follow up within the week (about three to four days later) and then about three to four days after that. And always have a call to action so they know what you want them to do.

I find it helpful to have a follow-up email template created in Gmail called Follow up 1, Follow up 2 and Follow up 3. (After 3 I suggest adding them to your quarterly update newsletter list, more on that below). The follow-up email should (subtly) answer these questions:

"Who are you, and when did we meet?"

"What were a couple of main points we discussed during the meeting?"

"Something you acknowledge or are grateful for in the meeting?"

"What's your suggested next step?"

"Why should I do it/What's in it for me?" - Here's the place to create what Yin calls 'credible urgency'- i.e. you have a Demo Day coming up, you've had second meetings with several investors, you're raising a smaller note, and there's X space left, etc. Don't say you're about to close the round unless you are! Investors talk to each other and if they find out you lied, bye bye funding and credibility."

After you go through your round of follow-ups, add them to your monthly/quarterly update list. Not the one you update your own investors on, but rather, your "interested parties" list. Make sure to share "knock your socks off" traction points, and be brief and bold. Don't be surprised if someday, a few months down the line, they respond and say "Hey! Long time! It looks like things are great - we should meet!" And play the game right along, come with confidence, no sour grapes please, and now YOU see if THEY'RE the right fit for YOU!

HANDLING REJECTION

This is going to be a hard time. It's like going on a series of blind dates every night for months, and rejection can be brutal. Please try not to take every rejection personally.

Going back to the theater metaphor for a moment, in a past life, I was acting in NYC, Off, and Off Off Broadway. (Yes, that is a thing ;)) That meant a constant stream of auditions and, with them, a steady stream of no's. It was hard not to tell myself that I was not a good actress and that it was all about me. Instead, I kept saying - "I wasn't the right fit for what the director had in mind." And when it was the right fit - it just clicked, and the part was mine!

This is also true with investors. They have a mental model of the companies they wish to invest in, what the founders should be like, what the traction should be, etc. Persuading Investors to break that model is challenging. Remember, you want a good fit as much as they do, so if it's a no, likely there's another investor who is a much better fit for you.

Investor "ghosting" can be very disheartening, especially if you heard the typical Silicon Valley ra, ra, ra after a meeting - "Excellent, amazing, awesome, love it - totally want to be a part of it." You leave the meeting on cloud nine, already imagining the money in the bank. And then - crickets. You never hear from them again.

The truth is, no investor wants to say a hard "no". In the moment, they likely were excited by you and meant the praise they doled out. So why the silent treatment? It could be many things - other opportunities that are a better fit, they're too busy, they like you, but you are a bit too early, or, to use another dating analogy - "They're just not that into you."

TIPS FOR PEAK PERFORMANCE PRESENTING

Some people are born great presenters - charismatic, clear, and convincing. I can think of a few off the top of my head - Bill Clinton, Martin Luther King Jr., and of course, in the Tech World - Steve Jobs, who gave some of the most impactful product launches and presentations ever. But was he always that good?

In the 1980's videos of the early Apple days, you can see Steve Jobs was a far cry from the polished, powerful orator we came to know him as. He had sweat stains on his shirt (this might explain why he moved to black turtlenecks), and he kind of rambled, but he had one thing going for him for sure - he was a natural-born storyteller. He knew how to captivate and make the audience laugh without slides by telling great stories. And when Steve had solid, powerful, structured presentations like the iPhone launch in 2007, nearly 30 years later, he was a completely different person. He had come into his own.

Not everyone is a born storyteller; not everyone is born a captivating speaker. The good news? This can be improved and honed with hard work. Here are some tips to up your presentation game:

It's not you - it's your story - sometimes we think, "it's not the story; it's me." I can promise you that most often - once your story has structure and focus, your presentation style will improve SIGNIFICANTLY.

What you can do: Make sure the story is structured, tight and in the correct flow. Make sure it's pointed at the right target audience and addresses the things they want to hear. Stick to the structure I have given you - I promise it works!

Don't improvise – Even actors have a script. You will rarely see an actor improvise lines in a film or on stage unless it's an improv show, which a business presentation or pitch is NOT. When my clients try to improvise what they'll say on each slide, they usually repeat everything about three times, em and um a lot, and look very underprepared. It's tough to know what to say in the moment, especially when it's high-stakes, such as an investor pitch meeting.

What you can do: When working with clients who are preparing a pitch or presentation, we script out the story in the speaker's notes on each slide and get super clear on what needs to be said. Mumbling and nerves will improve dramatically when you're not reaching for words.

But also - don't memorize – This might sound contradictory to the previous tip. Script, yes, but please, don't memorize the script – use it as a guideline. If you try to memorize and suddenly forget a word – it can throw you off track, leading to a complete blackout, especially if you're on stage at an event.

What you can do: You should read and reread, recite and re-recite the script in order to become so familiar with it that it's practically memorized, but not. Then the fun starts - you can play with it and make it seem like you're simply making it up on the spot, like a spontaneous, light conversation. It might sound counterintuitive , but it works- try it and see for yourself.

Be (the best version of) yourself – Sometimes well meaning colleagues will say things like "you need to be more animated." This often drives people to make their best impression of a used car salesman or a QVC seller (which then comes across as inauthentic). I see this often on Shark Tank, where a company is being pitched by a shrill, shrieking CEO that makes me want to cover my ears. I can bet that one of the pitch coaches said 'more energy,' and this was their interpretation of it. When we attempt to be someone we're not, we set ourselves up to fail. Instead, try to be your most authentic self with a good dollop of passion and animation.

What you can do: Try this exercise: record yourself, on your webcam or phone, pitching in your regular voice. (Please don't do this in front of a mirror or with the camera on selfie mode - way too self conscious.

Now, think about something that excites you – a sporting event, traveling to a new destination, dancing, skydiving - you get the picture. Take a moment, and imagine yourself doing that thing you love. Now, record yourself describing the exciting thing to someone who's never done it! Get them excited about it! How do you talk when you are passionate and enthusiastic about something?

Now, launch straight into your pitch while keeping that excitement and enthusiasm. Make sure to keep recording it!

Then, watch all the recordings. (Trust me, nobody likes watching themself recorded, but this is super important!) Is your pitch more animated after the "excitement story?" If your pitch can still use some more oomph, or you've gone too far over the top, try it another few times until you get the right level of authentic animation. Remember what it feels like to be at that level of excitement and let that same feeling live inside your body when you pitch. Believe it or not, it's the same adrenaline!

No "ums" or "buts" about it – Presenters often use a filler word like "um, like, ok, right, but." It gets used at the end of sentences or at every pause. Usually, people are entirely unaware of these filler words until I point them out or they see themselves recorded.

I call this the "Chronic Um." It's not a pause to search for a word we're forgetting; these are moments of our brain doubting what we're saying, questioning how we're coming across, and searching for approval. It's not the worst thing, but when there are so many of these filler words, it is simply distracting to listeners and dilutes your message's potency.

What you can do: If you want to get rid of these, ask a friend or a colleague to help - have them watch you present and when they hear you use a filler word, they should clap (by clap, I don't mean slap, bruise or electrocute, it's merely a way to draw your attention to it).

At first, you won't understand why they clapped. It will seem that they were just interrupting you. The second time they clap, you'll see that filler word as clear as day, and after a few claps, you'll start to notice your pattern and stop the "um" before it even slips out. Just like getting rid of any bad habit – awareness is the first step.

Practice does make perfect - Actors, singers, dancers, and athletes all go through intense rehearsal or practice periods before a show or game. Presenters often don't give themselves that privilege and come to a presentation without rehearsing it even once! Presentations need practice, especially when they're as crucial as an investor pitch. It's not enough just to read the presentation over, your whole body needs to run it through. We learn on a different level when reading than when doing.

What you can do: Practice in front of your team / spouse / kids / neighbors, even your Uber drivers (hey, they're being paid to be a captive audience!) and get their feedback. You can also record yourself and watch it back like in the best version of yourself exercise. Practice over and over again until you feel complete mastery. Like I could wake you up in the middle of the night and say 'pitch me' and you'd launch right into it. The more times you pitch, the more comfortable and polished you will be.

'Still feels like the first time' - If you give the same pitch, speech or presentation, again and again, it may start to feel old, stale and boring. You may start to tire of hearing your voice. But you must remember that the audience is seeing you for the very first time. It's not their fault that you're getting tired of presenting the same pitch over and over again; they deserve to be just as wowed as your first audience!

What you can do: Before each meeting or speech, take a moment to remember why you're doing this, what's at stake, what the first time felt like, and what a rush it was. Think that someone sitting in the room might be the person you've been waiting to meet, and you want to give it your all. Then go in there and slay it!

Even the most outstanding presenters spend a lot of time preparing their story and practicing it. In the book, Becoming Steve Jobs, the authors describe how intense his prep was. They note that "Steve would rehearse endlessly and fastidiously." We should all be doing the same.

THE ELEVATOR PITCH - BE READY TO PITCH IN A PINCH

Seneca once said that "Luck is where preparation meets opportunity." I genuinely believe that we can help move luck in our direction by being prepared for opportunity when it knocks. And one of the must-have tools in our storytelling arsenal is the infamous 'elevator pitch' - or the "Quick Pitch", as I have dubbed it. And you never know when the opportunity might knock - at a networking event, on an airplane, or even in line for coffee at Starbucks. If you find yourself conversing with someone who could be a potential investor/user/partner/connector - it is important to be ready to pitch them in a fast, powerful way.

I heard Susan Wojcicki, CEO of YouTube, speak a few years ago, and she said that it usually takes people about 15 minutes to explain to her what they do and what the value is. They've lost her if they can't do that in a minute. And Susan is not alone… in an age of pervasive ADHD and short form TikTok videos, if we haven't grabbed someone's attention in 30 seconds (some might argue 10), then we've blown the opportunity.

Just stating what you do or what your company does in complex or tedious terms can bring the conversation to a screeching - and awkward - halt. Let's tackle the preparation part in Seneca's timeless quote and have an elevator pitch ready.

The term 'elevator pitch' has come to mean how you would tell your story if you met someone super important and had a minimal amount of time to hook them, to ensure they wanted to continue the conversation (i.e. in an elevator). There are three elevator pitches that you should have handy, and here's how to get them ready to go:

The (Actual) Elevator Pitch - I coached the pitches for the Startupfest "Elevator World Tour," where 100 startups could pitch investors in an actual elevator competing for a sizable cash price. This has taken place in Paris, Toronto, Tel Aviv and more - and always in a very tall building, where the time from the ground floor to the top and down again was an average of one minute 26 seconds. For me, that's a good rule of thumb - have about a minute prepared, with room for about 30 seconds of Q & A.

What should be in it?

The problem you are solving + your solution + some staggering fact about the market or something amazing you've accomplished.

That's it! The hope is that you will have grabbed their interest, and now they are intrigued, asking questions and continuing the conversation.

The "Handshake" Pitch - (well, post-COVID we should probably call it the elbow bump pitch). This is what usually happens at a networking event. People milling around, chitchatting and the phrase "So what do you do?" is continuously repeated throughout the event. Here, you have about 20 seconds to grab their attention and make them want to continue the conversation.

The content? The beautiful part is that it is THE SAME as the elevator pitch - **Problem + Solution + Intriguing fact** - but condensed. And no - it's not your elevator pitch at warp speed; it's a shorter, yet powerful version at a normal, human speed.

The "Eyeblink" Pitch - Imagine that you were at a conference and see Mark Zuckerberg walking past you, and you have the perfect company for a Meta acquisition. Zuck's not going to stand around waiting as you hem and haw - you have to give him the bottom line up front - the hook. What does he stand to gain by associating with you? Have a short, powerful sentence that states what you do and, more importantly, the value it brings. I would create about six to seven different 'Eyeblinks' and have them ready to go to the right person at a moment's notice.

Try to find out who you're pitching to. The story will differ for a potential investor, a potential customer, or just a random person. Have a few different versions to make the villain more personal to the person you're speaking with. While an investor might be more interested in users' pain and how it will make money, a potential customer resonates more with their own pain and how your solution can help improve their lives. The overriding structure of the pitch would stay the same, but the story would change.

Think of your elevator pitches as a work in progress - you should have a running Google sheet shared with your team, constantly adding pitches that have worked for you to the list so everyone can benefit from them. Oh - and please make sure that EVERYONE on your team knows how to pitch your company in the best way possible - you never know if the next person you or they are going to meet can change your lives - so be prepared for the opportunity.

Q&A - It might be more important than the pitch!

When your startup is preparing for demo day, a pitch event or an investor meeting - countless hours go into preparing the pitch, getting the story "pitch perfect", and rehearsing till you know it frontwards and backwards. But, hand on your heart, how much time do you spend preparing for Q&A? Oh, you never prepare for that? Well, you must have a list of questions they'll ask you, right? Oh, no list? Well, you've come to the right place!

The good news is that people aren't terribly creative (even Investors :)), and it's easy to predict what questions you will be asked. So get prepared:

Make an Extensive Question List - List all the questions you've been asked, those you are pretty confident you will be asked and those you absolutely dread being asked (i.e. exit strategy, technological barriers, competition, etc.). Make a shared Google Drive document with your team and keep adding questions as they come up.

Categorize the Questions - Group questions by topic - financials, marketing, team, technology, etc. to make it easier to reference them.

Answer the Questions - Write down answers to all the questions until you feel comfortable answering them. No need to memorize them;

just familiarize yourself with them. If you don't know the answer, defer to the team member that can best answer it and have them fill in the blanks.

Review Before the Pitch - Just like you'd be looking over your pitch before a bid event or meeting, look over your Q & A. There is no need to memorize the answers; just know them well enough that it feels very natural to discuss difficult topics.

These questions are only the tip of the iceberg. Investors want to be sure that their money is well-spent and will bring them the coveted 10x or larger ROI. Naturally, this starts by ensuring your business operates successfully and shows the potential for even more growth. However, carefully considering how you can answer these and other pertinent questions will convince investors that you are worth their time and money.

Above all, keep your cool. Sometimes investors will purposely ask challenging questions to see how you deal with fire. You want to take it in stride, answer to the best and most credible of your ability, and also know when to say, "Great question - I don't have all the data in front of me - can I get back to you on that?" It's better than trying to make something up on the spot and getting caught off guard. Hey, and it gives you an excuse to continue the conversation and follow up by email!

As a bonus to my readers, I've gone ahead and compiled a list of the most common questions investors ask. They are grouped into question types. Feel free to grab the relevant questions, make the list and answer them. Obviously, there are many more questions; some are specific to your domain, so you can add as you go, but this is a good start:

QUESTIONS ABOUT YOUR COMPANY VISION:

1. What have you discovered (i.e. your fundamental insight) before everyone else?

2. What do you realize that defies conventional wisdom or understanding?

3. Are you creating a new category?

4. What is the historical evolution of your category?

5. What is your big vision?

6. What will it take to achieve the big vision?

Questions About the Company:

1. Where are you headquartered?

2. Do you have offices anywhere else?

3. How many employees do you have?

4. When and where did you incorporate?

Questions About the Problem:

1. What is the problem you're solving?

2. How do you know that it's a problem?

3. What are people currently doing to deal with this problem?

4. How much is this problem worth? (Value? Spend?)

5. Who are the audience/s that need the problem solved?

Questions About the Solution:

1. What is your solution?

2. What's unique about it?

3. How does it work?

4. Is it live?

5. Are people using it already?

6. Can you show me what it looks like?

7. Do you have a demo?

8. Can you tell me a user story?

9. Who loves your product? (Testimonials!)

10. How can I connect with five customers who have used your product or service?

11. What's the technology behind your solution?

12. Who developed it?

13. Do you have anything proprietary in the technology?

14. Why do users care about your solution?

15. What are the major product milestones?

16. What are the key differentiated features of your solution?

17. What are the key differentiated benefits of your solution?

18. What have you learned from early versions of the solution?

19. What are the two or three key features you plan to add?

20. What are additional products/offerings you plan to develop?

QUESTIONS ABOUT YOUR UNFAIR ADVANTAGE/SECRET SAUCE:

1. What's your secret sauce?

2. Is there anyone on the team with proprietary insight

that made this idea possible?

3. Is there anything patentable about the solution/technology?

QUESTIONS ABOUT YOUR VALUE PROPOSITION:

1. Whose lives do you make better?

2. What are their lives like before the use of your product?

3. What is their fundamental pain without you?

4. For those who pay you, what budget does the spend come out of? What spend do you replace?

5. Why will someone replace an existing spend by spending money with you?

6. Why will someone spend money with you now rather than wait?

Questions About Traction:

1. How far along are you?

2. What version of the product do you have?

3. Do you have a proof of concept? (POC)

4. Is there anything proprietary about it?

5. Have you filed a patent? When?

6. Are there any regulatory issues (i.e. FDA, ISO)?

7. If there are regulatory issues, what are you doing to be compliant?

8. Have you raised any funding so far?

9. Who's invested in you?

10. How much money have you invested yourself?

11. What traction has the company gotten (whatever is relevant to you).
    a. Sales
    b. Traffic to the company's website

    c.   Downloads

    d.   Daily active users (DAU)

    e.   Monthly active users (MAU)

    f.   Length of session

    g.   Returning users/repeat business

    h.   Engagement levels

QUESTIONS ABOUT MARKET SIZE/VALUE:

1. What is your available top-down market? (TAM)

2. What do you think represents the total served market of today? (SAM)

3. Who is serving this market right now?

4. If you define the customer as the person who pays you, what is the customer profile you cater to?

5. Why does your company have high growth potential?

6. What will your market look like after using your product or service in five years?

7. What is the market segment you're going after? Why are you starting there?

QUESTIONS ABOUT MARKET TRENDS AND OPPORTUNITIES:

1. Why are you doing this now?

2. What recent trends make this possible now?

3. What is the proof of these trends? (Reports, quotes, regulations, etc.)

4. How do you track trends in your market?

5. Why wasn't this possible five years ago?

6. Is there an inflection point in the market to leverage?

7. How will the business unfold over time?

QUESTIONS ABOUT GO TO MARKET:

1. What are your Go to Market strategies?

2. How are you acquiring customers now?

3. What is your Customer Acquisition Cost? (CAC)

4. What's the Lifetime Value of each client? (LTV)

5. What is the typical sales cycle between initial customer contact and the closing of a sale?

6. What have you tapped into that is causing so many users to sign up so quickly?

7. What percentage of the market do you plan to get over what period of time?

8. How did you arrive at the sales of your industry and its growth rate?

9. How do you plan to scale in the next 12 months?

10. What's your K Factor? (virality)

11. How are you going to close sales?

QUESTIONS ABOUT COMPETITION:

1. What if one of the more prominent players, e.g. Google, Meta, etc., launched a product/service just like yours? What would you do?

2. Who will the company's competitors likely be?

3.   What will your advantages be over them?

4.   What are your most defensible advantages today?

5.   What will contribute to increased defensibility in the
     next six months? The next twelve or eighteen months?

6.   Who could be your best partners and complementors
     in the market? Why might they have an incentive to
     help us hurt your competitors?

7.   What other companies or organizations benefit most if
     you are successful?

8.   What are your weakest competitive barriers?

9.   What gives you a unique competitive advantage?

10. What advantages do your competitors have over you?

11. Compared to your competition, how do you compete
     concerning price, features, and performance?

QUESTIONS ABOUT THE TEAM:

1. Who are the founders and key team members?

2. How long have the team members known each other?

3. Have team members worked together before?

4. Do you have a solid Founders' agreement in place?

5. What relevant domain experience does the team have?

6. What key additions to the team are needed in the short term?

7. Why is the team uniquely capable of executing the company's business plan?

8. How many employees do you have?

9. What motivates the founders?

10. How do you plan to scale the team in the next 12 months?

11. Can you scale up the volume without proportional

scaling up headcount?

QUESTIONS ABOUT THIS FUNDING ROUND:

1. Do you have a lead investor?

2. How much of the round have you secured?

3. Why are you raising money? Why not just bootstrap?

4. What will you achieve with the money? (Not how you will spend it!!)

5. What's your round objective? (similar question to the last one)

6. When will you close your round?

7. How far will the round get you?

8. How much runway (months) will you buy?

9. When will you need to raise more capital?

10. How much of your future growth can be funded through profitable revenues in the next 18 months

rather than raising additional equity?

11. If you were to raise enough to get to a breakeven with your cash flow, how much would you need?

12. How do you know the amount of money you need and, could you scale your business with less?

13. Why don't you build the business yourself without an investment?

14. Who else is interested?

15. Who else have you shown this to?

QUESTIONS ABOUT NEXT FUNDING ROUND:

1. What are the top three metrics/goals required for you to get to the next round of capital raise?

2. What key positions do you need to fill as you scale the business and to get to the next round of capital raise?

3. What would your scaled unit economics look like?

QUESTIONS ABOUT FINANCIALS:

1. What are the company's three-year projections?

2. What are the key assumptions underlying the projections?

3. How much equity and debt has the company raised?

4. What's the cap table structure?

5. What future equity or debt financing will be necessary?

6. How much of a stock option pool is being set aside for employees?

7. How much burn will occur until the company gets to profitability?

8. What are the key metrics that the management team focuses on?

9. Do you realize you're vastly underestimating your marketing expenses (or sales expense, or margins through channels, or headcount required for direct selling)?

10. Do you know comparable numbers for similar businesses?

11. What do the economics at a unit level look like now and at a steady state?

12. What are this sector's 'rules of thumb' for margins (gross, unit contribution, EBITDA)?

13. What are the key assumptions underlying your medium-term and steady-state projections?

QUESTIONS ABOUT PRODUCT/MARKET FIT:

1. What is the one thing above all else you must do to succeed?

2. Can you deliver only the value-add?

3. Who is the one competitor to position against in the market?

4. How will you get leveraged distribution?

QUESTIONS ABOUT RISK:

1. What do you see as the principal risks to the business?

2. What legal risks do you have?

3. Do you have any regulatory risks?

4. Are there any product liability risks?

5. How do you plan to mitigate these risks?

QUESTIONS ABOUT INTELLECTUAL PROPERTY (IP):

1. What key IP does the company have (patents, patents pending, copyrights, trade secrets, trademarks, domain names)?

2. What comfort do you have that the company's intellectual property does not violate the rights of a third party?

3. How was the company's intellectual property developed?

4. Would any prior employers of a team member have a

potential claim to the company's intellectual
property?

TRICKY QUESTIONS (AND SOME ANSWERS):

1. How did you come up with this idea?

2. If this (the venture being pitched) was to fail, what would you do next? (They really want you to answer that this is not an option cause you're not thinking about failure!)

3. What does success look like to you?

4. For women: Do you have a family / want to start a family – how will you focus on this? (Yes, I know that question sucks big time and is borderline illegal. But questions like this do come up, so it's advisable to have a nice, yet firm reply ready.)

5. What are the team's top hypotheses to test in the next few months?

6. What keeps you up at night?

7. What is the company's desired pre-money valuation?

(This is tricky because you probably shouldn't answer this right away – too high, you overshoot, too low, you undervalue…)

8. What is your exit strategy? (As I already stated in the 'Ask Slide' section, this is not something you should put on a slide or answer! Your answer should be to the effect of "We are fully focused on building a strong, lasting company. That's our core mission and passion." – They really want to hear that you're not looking for a quick sell!)

9. Who believes in you and how can I get in touch with them?

10. What entrepreneurs do you admire and why?

11. What mistakes have you made thus far in this business and what have you learned? (Failure and mistakes are an integral part of being a Founder! How you have dealt with it is what they really want to know about!)

12. What if three to five years down the road we think you're not the right person to continue running this company and we want to bring in an outside CEO — how will you deal with that? (The Founder/CEO is not always the best-suited person for the job. They want

to know that you have the company's best interests at heart and you won't put your ego first!)

13. Have you ever been fired from a job? Tell us about it. (What they really want to know here is how you challenged things, moved and shook – didn't stay put. How you dealt with challenges in a workplace says a lot about you.)

I know, I know, it's a lot! But trust me, the more prepared you are to answer these questions, the better you will come off to an Investor! And you might have noticed that many of these questions will have been answered if you go according to my deck format! Yes! Less work for you, more impressive for them!

Epic Pitch Fails - The biggest mistakes startups make - and what to do instead

Over the years, I've seen some startup fails that have made me cringe in pain for the founders, thinking, "No, they didn't!" I truly felt for them. I almost wished the ground would open up and swallow them because that would be less painful.

Over the years, several investors have candidly shared faux pas and red flags that they strongly recommend avoiding. Here are just a few painful moments and some suggestions for avoiding falling into the same traps. Identities have been changed to protect the innocent - and the not so innocent.

Epic Pitch Fail #1 - Not Doing Your Homework - Some startups try the 'spray and pray' method, sending cold emails, eventually getting a few meetings. Hey, it can work; some investors are more responsive to it than others. Others get introduced by a trusted connection, which merits a "yes" to a meeting. Either of these and many other methods are acceptable. Where's the fail? Not finding out anything about the investor before you ask for an intro, send an email or even before you meet.

The managing partner of a VC told me that one of his favorite questions is "So why do you think we're the right fit for you?" He's astounded by how many Founders hemmed and hawed without an answer. He goes even bolder - "What do you know about us?" - the answers are usually more hemming and hawing with a series of grunts.

How to Avoid Fail #1 - As I already stated in the section on preparing for a VC meeting, research the Investor/s BEFORE the meeting - look at their portfolio. Is there a potential collaboration with one of their portfolio companies? Emphasize this! Find trends and themes to their strategy and bring those up in an email or a meeting to show your knowledge and make them feel like you bothered to learn about them. Read their blog, find out what they are passionate about and mention that in a meeting. This should be a rule of thumb for any meeting, not just with investors.

Epic Pitch Fail #2 - Talking Trash - A VC Partner told me about a time she asked a team about their competition; specifically one pretty direct competitor and the CEO answered, "Oh, they are no competition for us, they suck at what they do." She smiled a bit sheepishly and then told them that she was on their Advisory Board, not as an investor, but as someone who had extensive industry knowledge about their field and thought they were actually quite good. The CEO turned a few different shades of red, and needless to say, the meeting was over. Could the CEO have known this before? Maybe… but there's a better way to avoid it:

How to Avoid Fail #2 - As discussed in the competition section, don't EVER diss your competition! Ever! You never know who knows who, who's connected to whom. Stay factual - "Well, Competitor X does ABC and is doing quite well with it, based on the $15 million round they just closed. We also do ABC but with a different approach, set of tools, and method. This enables us to also do XYZ…"

Play off your competitors' strengths to highlight your strengths and then stress your points of differentiation.

Epic Pitch Fail #3 - TMI - A prominent Angel Investor told me that one of his pet peeves is when a company voluntarily puts their valuation on their pitch deck. "It's one thing if I ask them about it," he said, "and there's a particular answer I'm looking for. But why shoot yourself in the foot and offer a valuation that might be much lower or higher than what I'm thinking? This should be a conversation much later in the due diligence process." Exit strategies are another thing not to volunteer, as I also already explained in the "Ask Slide" section.

How to Avoid Fail #3 - Never volunteer your valuation or exit strategy. And don't put them on a slide! Rob Go, also an investor, writes that the market will dictate your valuation; you should wait to talk numbers. First, get them interested in you, and excited, and then you can go for a higher valuation - not too shockingly high. If you get pushback, you can always come down on your numbers.

Top Epic Pitch Fail of All Time - Arguing with an Investor...I had prepped a group of finalists for a prestigious pitch competition with a hefty prize. One of them gave a truly memorable pitch - it seemed he had the win in the bag. Then came the Q&A. An Investor on the judging panel asked a question that was, in all truth, a bit snarky. Instead of breathing, smiling and answering, the Founder started arguing with him, proving him wrong, leaving the other judges shifting uncomfortably in their seats. I was so embarrassed and disappointed. The last thing you want to do is to come across as uncoachable and argumentative.

How to Avoid this - Don't argue, just don't. Even if the Investor said something completely off-kilter, say, "thanks for the feedback; I will check it out." Even if you're ready to scream! And then, when you've calmed down a bit, see if there's anything of value to be taken from their comments. Usually, as much as we hate to admit it, there is! And that's a great reason to follow up with them and start a conversation - thank them for their insight, tell them what you plan to do with it and maybe ask for a meeting to hear more advice.

You have to understand that investors, especially in Silicon Valley, often know each other and compare notes - if you blow it with one, the word might get out. So leave them smiling, not cringing, even if they aren't the right match for you - they might have a friend who is, so be sure to end on a high note.

Final Thoughts - What's the Future of Storytelling for Startups

As a storyteller for startups, I often wonder if Artificial Intelligence (AI) will eventually take over my job. After all, machines are now able to do many things that were once considered the domain of humans. But when it comes to writing, I'm not so sure. Sure, there are already programs that can generate basic text. But in my opinion, they lack the creativity and insight that humans bring to the table.

Enter Generative Pretrained Transformer 3 (GPT-3), a state-of-the-art language processing model developed by OpenAI. You would have to be living in a cave not to hear about the hype that their open source tool, ChatGPT is generating. (Go ahead, try it yourself- It's mind-blowing!)

GPT-3 is one of the largest and most powerful language models ever created, with 175 billion parameters. GPT-3 is trained on a massive amount of text data and is able to generate human-like text in a variety of styles and formats. It is commonly used for natural language processing tasks such as language translation, text summarization, and question answering, among others. GPT-3 has been praised for its ability to generate high-quality text, but it has also raised concerns about the potential for it to be used for malicious purposes, such as the generation of fake news.

GPT-3 is still in its early stages, but it has already shown promise. In one experiment, it was used to automatically generate a summary of a complex legal document. The results were impressive, and the system was able to accurately capture the main points of the document.

As text generators become more sophisticated, they will become even more useful for a variety of tasks. In the future, they could be used to create entire documents from scratch, or to automatically translate between languages.

While AI systems may be able to assist humans in the storytelling process, it is unlikely that they will be able to fully replace human storytellers in the foreseeable future. AI technology has advanced significantly in recent years. And while it is now capable of generating text that is difficult for humans to distinguish from text written by other humans, storytelling is a complex and nuanced art that involves more than just the ability to generate text.

Storytelling involves creating a narrative that engages and captivates an audience, and this requires a level of creativity, empathy, and emotional intelligence that AI systems currently lack. Additionally, storytelling often involves drawing on personal experiences and emotions, which AI systems are not capable of doing.

So how does AI affect the future of storytelling for startups and pitch decks? On the one hand, AI technology has potential to help startups create better pitch decks in several ways. For example, AI-powered natural language processing (NLP) tools can be used to help identify and highlight key information and insights within large datasets, making it easier for startups to identify potential investors, and tailor their pitch decks to their specific needs and goals.

AI-powered text generation technology can also be used to assist in the creation of the pitch deck itself. By analyzing large amounts of text data, AI systems can learn to generate text in a variety of styles and formats, and can be used to help startups create compelling and persuasive narratives that are more likely to engage and persuade potential investors.

Additionally, AI technology can be used to help optimize the layout and design of pitch decks, using machine learning algorithms to identify the most effective combinations of images, text, and other elements to create visually appealing and easy-to-understand presentations.

Pitch decks of the future are likely to involve a greater emphasis on using technology to create immersive and engaging experiences for audiences. This could include the use of virtual reality, augmented reality, and other forms of interactive media to bring stories to life in new and exciting ways.

Having said all that, creating a successful investor deck is a complex task that involves more than just generating text. It also involves understanding the needs and goals of the investors, creating a compelling narrative, and presenting information in a clear and concise manner.

While GPT-3 may be able to assist in the process of creating an investor deck, it is unlikely that it would be able to produce a successful deck on its own without human input and guidance. Ultimately, the success of an investor deck will depend on the ability of the startup team to effectively communicate their vision and persuade investors to invest in their company.

It is difficult to predict exactly when AI technology will be advanced enough to allow founders to create investor decks without human input. The development of AI technology is advancing rapidly; and new and more powerful AI systems are being developed all the time.

It is likely that AI systems will continue to improve and be able to assist in the process of creating investor decks, but it is unlikely that they will be able to replace human involvement completely in the foreseeable future. It will ultimately depend on the specific goals and needs of the startup team, as well as the state of AI technology at the time. As the use of AI and NLP technologies continues to advance, we may see the development of new tools and platforms that make it easier for startups to create and share compelling stories with their audiences.

OK - up until now, this chapter was written 90% by ChatGPT and Jasper.ai. Pretty astonishing, huh?

Granted, I had to feed them all kinds of points to generate disparate pieces of content that I wove together into a fleshed-out chapter. But as I watched ChatGPT and Jasper.ai spit out the content, I must admit that I was mesmerized.

How is this different from the research I did for the book and the sources I brought in and then pieced together and edited? It's faster, more comprehensive and pretty darn well put together.

Am I nervous about being replaced? Well, as I told someone who asked me if, in this book - am I giving away all of my secrets? Will people now not need my services because I literally have just handed you, on a silver platter, all of my secret formulas, tips and tricks?

The answer is, no. Just like when a chef publishes their top recipes in a cookbook - some people will gladly make the recipe at home and feel thrilled that they're eating a chef's meal, while others will now more than ever want to come to eat from the chef's table. And since there's only one of me, those 'diners' will continue to fill my schedule each day, astounding me with their incredible innovation, and granting me the honor and pleasure of helping craft their pitch.

The hard part is to explain your idea simply and show your true differentiation - this will be around for a while. But maybe after doing that, you could use an AI technology that has scanned thousands of pitch decks to take your idea, ask you some questions, and create a full deck. It could create texts, images, and maybe even a deep fake video of you or someone else explaining or narrating the deck and perhaps the most important thing, help you change the deck or the story or messages according to the Investor's past investments or interest? Wow, the possibilities!

This technology would be amazing because it helps entrepreneurs with great ideas but doesn't have the time or resources to create a professional-looking pitch deck. Also, it would help ensure that all the important information is included and that the story is engaging and differentiated. AI gives us a set of game-changing tools for entrepreneurs seeking funding.

Ultimately, the future of storytelling for startups will likely involve combining traditional storytelling techniques and cutting-edge technology.

I don't see AI replacing storytellers like me, just yet. I don't know if AI will ever be able to replace human creativity completely. At the end of the day, we are the ones who created AI in the first place. But it can help us become more efficient and productive. After all, a good chef has many sous chefs that execute in a fancy kitchen. In the next couple of years, I'm sure we'll have an AI assistant as part of the process, making us better or giving us a range of versions to choose from with messages, slides, styles, and clarifications. It's going to be an exciting future.

I, too, look forward to having an AI 'sous chef' (or a few) of my own - to save me time and free my unique resources up for what my own personal human AI loves and does best - write other people's stories.

ABOUT THE AUTHOR

For over 20 years, world renowned
Corporate Storyteller and Pitch
Alchemist Donna Griffit has roamed the
globe working with over 1000 Startups,
Fortune 500 companies and Venture
Capitalists in a wide variety of
industries.

Donna has consulted and trained clients in over 30 countries, helping
them create, edit and deliver verbal and written presentations, pitches
and messages that sing.

Donna has the ability to magically spin raw data into compelling stories
that have raised over $1.5B.

Give Donna your numbers, your facts, your figures, your bits and bytes
and she will put them all through her magic filter and spin them into a
golden story. Yes - where you see data - Donna sees a living, breathing,
captivating story with the potential to drive people to action. And
that's what good storytelling is all about - not showing how good you
are rather how great you can make them!

Donna's sincere belief is that everyone has a story that is unique and compelling. There are no boring stories – there are merely layers and stacks of information piled up, obscuring the beauty of the story. Let Donna help peel the layers away and let you polish your stories until it "shines like the top of the Chrysler building."

Donna Grifft
Corporate Storyteller and Pitch Alchemist
https://www.donnagriffit.com/
https://www.linkedin.com/in/donnaabraham

Get a free copy of my Ultimate Investor Cheat Sheet at https://www.donnagriffit.com/ or scan the QR Code below:

References:

The Importance of Storytelling

https://www.ynharari.com/book/sapiens-2/

https://www.wordsalive.org/blog/2018/9/5/the-history-of-storytelling

https://reporter.rit.edu/tech/evolution-storytelling

https://www.verywellmind.com/how-do-false-memories-form-2795349

Principle of Chunking -

https://thepeakperformancecenter.com/educational-learning/thinking/chunking/chunking-as-a-learning-strategy/

https://www.interaction-design.org/literature/book/the-glossary-of-human-computer-interaction/chunking

https://guykawasaki.com/the-only-10-slides-you-need-in-your-pitch/

The Why:

https://www.freshworks.com/crm/sales/summary-of-start-with-why-blog/#Chapter3

A note about the slides

https://hbr.org/2012/10/do-your-slides-pass-the-glance-test

https://www.today.com/health/your-brain-cant-swipe-hear-same-time-scans-show-t60356

https://guykawasaki.com/the-only-10-slides-you-need-in-your-pitch/

https://medium.com/adventures-in-consumer-technology/this-is-how-we-make-slides-at-apple-b8a84352bf6d

Uber for X:

https://www.theatlantic.com/business/archive/2016/02/adam-grant-originals-uber-for-x/459321/

http://reidhoffman.org/linkedin-pitch-to-greylock/

Traction: https://www.washingtonpost.com/business/on-small-business/how-to-pitch-your-company-mark-cuban-fellow-startup-investors-share-their-secrets/2013/08/26/7fbc2596-0e88-11e3-85b6-d27422650fd5_story.html

http://www.startupdefinition.com/vanity-metrics

https://techcrunch.com/2011/07/27/founder-office-hours-schedit/

Market Size and Whys

http://reidhoffman.org/linkedin-pitch-to-greylock/   (Move   to Feed the FOMO)

http://articles.bplans.com/tam-sam-and-som-huh/

Go To Market -

http://articles.bplans.com/tam-sam-and-som-huh/

https://en.wikipedia.org/wiki/Growth_hacking

https://www.pendo.io/glossary/product-led-growth/

Competition -

http://www.entrepreneur.com/article/253341

http://www.gartner.com/technology/research/methodologies/research_mq.jsp

http://blogs.berkeley.edu/2013/11/11/a-new-way-to-look-at-competitors/

https://www.startups.co/articles/analyzing-startup-business-competitors

Business Model

Strategyzer.com

https://en.wikipedia.org/wiki/Business_Model_Canvas

https://fi.co/insight/the-10-most-popular-startup-revenue-models

https://www.universitylabpartners.org/blog/7-different-business-model-ideas-for-your-startup

https://www.investopedia.com/terms/e/ebitda.asp

Opportunization

https://www.eisenhower.me/eisenhower-matrix/

http://reidhoffman.org/linkedin-pitch-to-greylock/

https://medium.com/@bchesky/7-rejections-7d894cbaa084

https://www.bvp.com/anti-portfolio

https://www.simon-kucher.com/sites/default/files/studies/Simon-Kucher_Global_Sustainability_Study_2021.pdf

https://sustainlab.co/blog/4-key-sustainability-legislation-you-should-know-about-in-2022

Team

https://www.stagevp.com/blog/2021/7/7/elevating-the-team-slide-in-any-pitch-deck

How to get VC meetings

https://en.wikipedia.org/wiki/Move_fast_and_break_things

http://blog.elizabethyin.com/post/149611764515/how-should-you-follow-up-with-an-investor

Peak Performance Presenting

https://www.amazon.com/Becoming-Steve-Jobs-Evolution-Visionary/dp/0385347421

Elevator Pitch

https://www.allegisgroup.com/en/insights/blog/2017/march/luck-is-when-preparation-meets-opportunity#:~:text=Roman%20philosopher%20Seneca%20once%20said,fast%2Dtracked%20promotion%20%E2%80%93%20nothing%20enables

https://www.elevatorworldtour.com/

Epic Fails

https://shockwaveinnovations.com/2014/02/16/answering-the-exit-strategy-question/

https://techcrunch.com/2015/04/28/sneaky-questions-early-stage-vcs-ask-founders-and-the-hidden-meaning-behind-each/

Future of Storytelling

https://openai.com/blog/chatgpt/

Made in the USA
Las Vegas, NV
03 April 2023

70095881R00118